Valuing and Investing in Equities

CROCI: Cash Return on Capital Investment

Valuing and Investing in Equities

in Equities

CROCI: Cash Return on Capital Investment

Francesco Curto

ELSEVIER

ACADEMIC PRESS
An imprint of Elsevier

*Francesco Curto is the Head of the CROCI Investment Valuation Group and the Head of the Research House at DWS, one
of the world's leading asset managers.*

*The views expressed in this book are the author's own views and are not the views of any of DWS Group GmbH & Co.
KGaA or any of its affiliated companies ("DWS Group").*

*The information and opinions contained in this document are for information and discussion purposes only, do not
constitute a financial promotion or do not purport to be fully complete. Whilst the author has used his best efforts to
ensure the accuracy or completeness of any information continued herein, no reliance may be placed for any purpose on the
information or opinions contained in this book for their accuracy or completeness. No representation, warranty or
undertaking, express or implied, is given as to the accuracy or completeness of the information or opinions contained in this
book and no liability accepted for the accuracy or completeness of any such information or opinions.*

*This book does not constitute or form part of any offer to issue or sell, or any solicitation of any offer to subscribe or
purchase, any shares or any other interests or services nor shall it or the fact of its distribution form the basis of, or be
relied on in connection with, any contract thereof. This book is not intended to constitute, and should not be construed as,
investment advice or as an offer, solicitation or recommendation of any financial instruments.*

CROCI© is a registered trademark of DWS Group.

British Library Cataloguing-in-Publication Data
A catalogue record for this book is available from the British Library

Library of Congress Cataloging-in-Publication Data
A catalog record for this book is available from the Library of Congress

ISBN: 978-0-12-813848-9

For Information on all Academic Press publications
visit our website at https://www.elsevier.com/books-and-journals

Publisher: Brian Romer
Editorial Project Manager: Susan Ikeda
Production Project Manager: Sujatha Thirugnana
                Sambandam
Cover Designer: Laurianne Poirier

Typeset by MPS Limited, Chennai, India

Working together
to grow libraries in
developing countries

www.elsevier.com • www.bookaid.org

To Chantal, Nicolas, Emanuel and Béatrice.
To my mother, Cosima, and my sisters, Giovanna, Anna, Daniela.
To Italy and Salento, that I miss more than I can say.
To my friends, 'fore te capu'.

Letter to the reader

Dear reader,

CROCI® is a DWS Group trademark that stands for Cash Return on Capital Invested. The acronym refers to a valuation technique used for research and investments. It was coined by a group of friends who arrived at DB in the mid-1990s. Back then, the single European financial market was still in the making, and so comparing valuations of companies across Europe was a challenge. CROCI enabled full comparability across sectors and markets, providing an excellent basis for market analysis and investments.

In the early days, the team spent what now seems like an endless number of meetings explaining how we adjust valuation and why. Confusion was the norm, and the most common question was "why?" Why do you go through so much pain? Why do you make this adjustment? Our answer was to highlight the errors of traditional approaches and explain why adjustments to valuations were required. Now the answer is different: "we do this because it is what you would do if you were buying a company with your own money". That is the simple reality: the moment that you consider buying a listed stock, you are about to buy a piece of a company. If you buy a piece of a company, then you perform due diligence on its accounts, making the necessary adjustments to ensure a proper economic basis for valuing the company. Some companies are easy to analyse, others are more complicated, and others still are impossible. If the latter is the case, then you move on to the next one. This is what you would do if you were buying the company with your own money. As agents we ought to do the same. Once you have a proper basis for comparing valuations, how should you build an investment strategy? How should you analyse the market? Or the economy? Within this book, I take the reader through this journey.

This is the frame of mind that people should be in when reading this book. At the beginning and at the end of the process, there is an investor who has some capital and is expecting a return. There are similarities between CROCI and Alice in Wonderland. Once you go through the looking glass, it is difficult to go back to the old ways. Whatever is your journey, I hope you enjoy this book!

Kind regards
Francesco Curto

Contents

Section 3
Through the looking glass

Foreword

Francesco Curto's *Valuing and Investing in Equities* takes readers through his career as an investor who steadfastly advises and practices disciplined valuation. He writes about his professional journey at Deutsche Bank and then DWS, while showcasing the valuation technique at the foundation of his investment philosophy and analysis for over 20 years, a technique called Cash Return on Capital Invested (CROCI).

He demonstrates the great importance of the CROCI metric throughout this book. He explains how CROCI quantifies the economic success of a company and how such an assessment is crucial to intrinsic valuation. CROCI is more precise in measuring capital invested and the income that it generates than other return on capital metrics, owing to both its calculation and its many adjustments to reported accounting figures. However, the CROCI analysis presented throughout this book on companies from all over the world shows that CROCI is much more than a metric or even a valuation technique. It is an analytical framework grounded in the concept of assessing the use of capital to determine whether shareholder value was enhanced. Investors cannot assess the future potential of any business unless they fully understand its past.

Francesco generously shares details of the CROCI framework and lessons learned from its application over the past two decades with readers as if repaying a debt from being fortunate enough to be introduced to such a conceptually sound and profitable analytical framework early on in his career by esteemed colleagues and mentors. He has taken this entrusted wisdom and lead a team dedicated to improving and broadening the use of the CROCI framework for investment strategies at DWS. CROCI is an analytical tool and an investment strategy that once an investor has in their collection, they only wish they had it sooner.

Rigorously assessing the productive use of resources is the spirit of CROCI. Investors now consider all resources that an enterprise might use. Resources include capital, intellectual property, interaction with society and environmental conservation. Analytical frameworks such as CROCI, brilliant minds like Francesco's and books like this one will help investors and all of us find our way.

Read this book and keep it on your shelf.

David Bianco, CFA
DWS Americas CIO
DWS Group, New York

Preface

I was certainly confused when I first arrived at Deutsche Bank in September 1998 after some real-life experiences: my family business, a good undergraduate degree in Business Economics, an excellent postgraduate education and some time as Research Fellow in a business school. Notwithstanding this solid background, it still took me a few years to make sense of the world of equity investment. Joining a sell-side organisation at the beginning of the biggest valuation bubble in living memory certainly didn't help, but I think I was probably not alone in struggling.

I arrived in Equity Research in the depths of the Emerging Markets crisis (the first of many crises in my professional career), and I was faced with a difficult choice. Which research team I should join: Semiconductor, Pharmaceutical, Chemicals, or Equity Strategy? In the end, I clicked with a Frenchman by the name of Pascal Costantini who was to become my mentor and dear friend. As the European Strategist, he collaborated in developing two valuation models. One was called Running The Numbers; the other, more advanced, was called Cash Return on Capital Invested (CROCI).

CROCI[1] was designed to enable full comparability across sectors and markets. Miko Giedroyc had long been working on using valuation to analyse equity markets—the papers he wrote around that time are still treasured in our vaults. Meanwhile, Pascal brought the magic touch. He defined the framework and the discipline. Their idea was to use CROCI both as a differentiating factor for stock pickers and also as an input in a bottom-up equity market approach.

This approach provided an interesting contrast to the sort of methodologies coming to light in the 1999 TMT bubble. Dot.com companies were valued using Enterprise Value-to-"Click"—in other words, valuation on the basis of the number of clicks received by a given website. Forget about earnings or revenues. This new valuation ratio was interested only in *potential* revenue generation. Think of valuing a shoe company based on how many steps people take in the shop. Characteristic of the period, EV/click came and went, but when someone left CROCI to join the technology team and a food manufacturing analyst became a software analyst, I felt as though

---

1. I will use CROCI and CROCI© are interchangeable throughout the book. Note that CROCI is a DWS trademark associated to a proprietary methodology developed for valuing companies. All rights are reserved.

I were a dying breed. Sometimes, though, one needs to trust one's instincts—my contrarian nature has always made me sceptical of fashions. And in due course, things started to fall into place and my confusion about equity investment faded away. In 2004, CROCI was used for the first time as a method for investing directly in the market and since 2013 the team has been part of DWS.[2] Twenty years on and here I am, writing a book about two decades of CROCI.

CROCI is, in its strictest sense, a valuation technique. However, CROCI has, over time, become a way of life, a holistic approach to investment in listed securities. I analyse companies, sectors and markets using the CROCI mindset; I look at how the economy works through the CROCI mindset; I think about how investments should be built and managed using the CROCI mindset; I think of what the final investor and client should want in terms of service and returns using the CROCI mindset; I even gave a presentation recently on geopolitics using this framework. CROCI simply permeates everything I do professionally. This holistic approach has limits and there are several other approaches for analysing the world of equities, but I believe that it comes closest to what equities ought to represent.

So what should the book focus on? I have given a lot of thought to this. I have spoken to Pascal, to my colleagues, to my clients. I even went to Greece to seek inspiration from the muses. Within this book, I share *with the reader the CROCI framework for valuing and investing in equities.* Valuing and investing in equities in theory ought to be simple, but in practice is a real muddle. The more you look at it, the more you get confused by the complexity of the environment, which is populated by both active and passive, investors and speculators; regulators, multiple layers of intermediaries between the company and the final investors, the media and several academic theories.

There was a risk, as I endeavoured to write this book, that I would have ended muddying the water by trying to cover too many issues. I weighed the option of just focusing on valuation or on investment. I decided to combine the issues as valuation and investment ought to be seen as the two side of the same coin and too many errors are generated by trying to separate the issues. I hope that readers will find the eclectic approach helpful. If have succeeded, then this book ought to be useful to practitioners, professionals, investors, consultants, students and academics.

The book is divided into three sections. Valuation, Investment and Through the Looking Glass. They follow a brief introduction that reviews the challenges that investors face and the context to them. Chapter 1, Investment and valuation, introduces the three sections, it defines the framework and analyses the pillars of an investment process: *capital and returns.*

---

2. The DWS Group is majority owned by Deutsche Bank AG.

Section 1 is about valuation, the basis of an investment process. The challenges for investors start early as data used for valuation is not defined by investors but by accountants and you discover that there is on average a 50% difference in valuation if you use accounting data rather than economic/investment data (Chapter 2: Valuing non-financial companies). You also discover that valuation is the net result of two factors (earnings and discount rate) that can both mutate and there appears not to be an obvious framework for either (Chapter 4: Stock picking based on economic fundamentals). Even when you define such framework, you deal with an industry that is telling you all about one of the variable (earnings) but only about the next 2 years, which has only 20% impact on valuation (Chapter 4: Stock picking based on economic fundamentals). Starting from first principles, I provide how CROCI defines a clear framework for valuing equities and provide tangible examples to help the reader.

Section 2 is about investing in equities. Valuation has historically been used by stock pickers to select the most attractive companies to invest in. I start by describing the challenges that stock pickers face and focus on how CROCI has been used as a systematic framework for investing in equities.

In Section 3, I discuss how CROCI is used as a basis for fundamental research on equities. It is a cry for help to the academic world. Over the past few years, I have come across a number of simple issues where our analysis had something very different to say. "Through the looking glass" is a reference to the novels by Lewis Carroll.[3] In the journey towards a better understanding of valuation, capital and return, I have traversed the looking glass and there is no easy way back. In this section, I focus on two issues: how inflation distorts the long-term valuation of equities and bubbles in equities as a way to discuss the need for more and better fundamental research on equities.

In the concluding Chapter 11, Odysseus on valuing and investing in equities, I summarise the main points that ought to be remembered when valuing and investing.

---

3. (Alice's Adventures in Wonderland, 1865; and "Through the looking glass", and what Alice found there, 1871).

Acknowledgements

I have always enjoyed research and because of that moving to Finance was not an obvious choice for me back in 1998. Now, with the benefit of hindsight, I could reflect on this as one of the best decisions I could have taken. I have been able to carry on research throughout my professional career and develop my learning.

It would be fair to say that I landed in possibly the best team. There are things that cannot be rationally explained and this is where luck kicks in. I was certainly lucky to land in the CROCI team. Although I was not able to work for long with Miko, Pascal welcomed me and was my mentor for a decade. It has been a great personal and working relationship at many levels. His uncompromising attitude and disdain for noise have helped me more than I can say. If this is my book and present my interpretation of CROCI, it certainly would have not happened without them.

CROCI has now evolved into a team that does not depend on individuals anymore. It is a collective approach to valuing and investing in equities and nothing would have been possible without the contribution of everyone working in the team. This is a fully integrated framework starting from first principles, moving to the analysis of companies, doing fundamental research, and defining investment strategies. A lot of work is required and that demands a fine structure behind it. If Pascal and Miko gifted us with their visions of CROCI; Virginie Galas, Colin McKenzie, and Mital Parekh helped to make it. They remain my most senior colleagues and deserve a special mention. Markus Barth, Joe Hall, Chris Town, and Janet Lear are no longer in CROCI but have helped to make the team as it is today. Sarvesh Agrawal and Dirk Schlueter have been very loyal for years and together with the entire Mumbai team (Bharat, Mukarram, Venkat, Vikash, Yogi, and the more recent joiners) are the cornerstone of what CROCI is today. They have endless patience in providing support to all that is done and will ensure a sound future for CROCI. Michael Yakir, Lynn Mulligan, Annie Bullock, and Gina Niehaus make sure the CROCI machinery keeps working smoothly and I can never thank them enough for it. Each deserves a special acknowledgement for everything they have and continue to do.

CROCI, as a process, is best suited for a fiduciary business and I have been (again) lucky to be part of the DWS Group (majority-owned by the DB

Group) since 2013. A special mention goes to Stefan Kreuzkamp, a man of few words, who trusted and helped me to become a wiser manager.

Finally, I wish to thank Scott Bentley, who scouted me and encouraged me to write this book. Without his patience and guidance throughout the past few years, this book would not be published.

Introduction

The *real* investor, a connoisseur of financial markets

Cecil Graham: What is a cynic?
Lord Darlington: A man who knows the price of everything, and the value of
nothing.
Cecil Graham: And a sentimentalist, my dear Darlington, is a man who sees
an absurd value in everything and doesn't know the market price of any single
thing.

(Oscar Wilde, Lady Windermere).

What Oscar Wilde never defined was the person who knows the price of an asset and its intrinsic value. Given his bohemian attitude, he might have called that person *a connoisseur of markets*. My preference is for 'the real investor', the person who has an intrinsic knowledge of the three cornerstones of investing: the price of an asset, its value and everything that may affect them. I add the term *real* to *investor* to distinguish it from its common definition, any participant in financial markets. I believe that being an investor requires sound judgement of the difference between price and value. Simply buying a financial asset does not make someone an investor, but the owner of a financial asset whose intentions need to be established. The acquisition of a financial asset could be for speculative purposes or for investment purposes. Adding 'real' removes any ambiguity. It is clear then that I am referring to a *competent* and *experienced* market operator, deeply aware of the difference between *price* and *value* as well as *everything that affects them.*

Investment and speculation

This attention to detail may sound fussy, but it is of fundamental importance. To clarify, let's compare an investor with a speculator. If, strictly speaking, an investor is interested in the difference between the price paid and the value received, then a *speculator* is someone only interested in making money through arbitrage between the price paid and the price received. That is to say, the focus of a speculator is strictly on 'price'. A speculator knows that an event is taking place and assumes that it will have an impact on prices, so she takes a position that takes advantage of it. Given the nature of markets and how fast prices can change, speculators tend to be on high alert — their time frame is generally short.

For *investors*, assessing the value of a company and its fundamentals is of primary importance. Investors need to undertake a time-consuming preliminary analysis that, once finalised, requires less monitoring than speculation does. Such investors focus solely on valuation and ignore relative performance. Unfortunately true investors are a rare breed. There are different factors driving equities (value, growth, momentum, size, liquidity, volatility, etc.), and ignoring other factors and focusing just on valuation may sometimes lead to a prolonged period of poor relative performance. The net result is that investors less extreme in their views can become stuck in the middle of the spectrum.

Where would you put yourself?

Where would you put yourself?

	1	2	3	4	5	
Investor						Speculator

Five typologies of market participants

I propose five broad types of market participants.

Number one is the real investor who focuses strictly on value, ignoring short-term price dynamics and performance relative to a benchmark. Due diligence is aimed at properly understanding a company's valuation. Assuming conditions do not change, there will be no change to the decision, irrespective of relative performance.

The second position describes typical professional investors. Valuation is fundamental, but other factors enter the decision-making process. Investments (stocks purchased and amounts) are made relative to a benchmark. Absolute performance is the objective, but poor relative performance can lead to changes in stocks and weights.

The third group combines elements of valuation and speculation while buying companies (Value and Momentum). It is possibly the largest group of market participants. Valuation is the anchor but there is much attention to short-term dynamics and how they may affect equity prices.[1] In this group, we see a more active role being played by media, brokers and traders.

(Continued)

---

1. While much attention is given to growth and momentum factors, our analysis indicates that there is no long term alpha in such factors.

(Continued)

Speculators in the fourth group may decide to look at valuation as a comfort factor but they mostly ignore it.

Those in group 5 are pure speculators who have no space for valuation in their framework.

Since you are reading this book the likelihood is that you fall somewhere between levels 1 and 3.

Investment is a social and not an exact science

If value and price matter, a solid understanding of the wider context and sociopolitical backdrop is also important. Take the example of State Owned Enterprises in many Emerging Markets. They often trade on attractive valuation ratios, but it is unclear whether their investment decisions are for the benefit of the broader interest of the society rather than their minority shareholders. Understanding governance also matters. As a shareholder, you are the owner of a small part of the company, but management often operates without considering your interests. This occurs either because investors are unaware of their rights or because they see equities as speculative rather than something to be held for the long term.[2]

At a practical level, the best investors are able to capture how external factors may end up affecting equities. This is why I believe that the real investor is either a connoisseur of markets or one in the making. She has possibly gone through a few business cycles and witnessed bubbles and depressions. The world of investment is like the world of good wood and wine: it gets better over time as the best investors are persistent. She makes mistakes and learn from them.

The education of an investor

If the world of investment is complex, the average investor is perhaps not well prepared to face it. Information about investment opportunities is widely available, and the Internet provides easier access to investment platforms than ever before. Even so, knowledge about equity investing among the general public and even for some financial professionals is poor. And, to many, the world of investment is full of ambiguity and unnecessary complexity.

---

2. Lack of good governance is a concern. One would expect improvements in the level of governance, but in fact, progresses have been patchy. I see poor practice taking hold in the Anglo-Saxon world, where a number of companies listed during the past decade have restrictive covenants defined by the founders. These limit shareholders' rights to such an extent that even a majority shareholder cannot take important decisions regarding the company.

Take the example of the 2008 financial crisis. In its aftermath, there were discussions about limiting the role of finance in our society. Protesters objected to the financialisation of the world economy. Some regulations have been introduced since then to curb unnecessary risks and to protect investors. But the level of education of the average investor has not changed.

There seems to be a tacit assumption that the level of financial knowledge should have increased along with wealth over the past centuries. But wealth does not beget investing. It is perhaps ironic that a capitalist system does not teach the basics of capitalism. People are taught about geography, civic education, sexual education, religious education and domestic education, but we are all supposed to understand investment innately. Higher education in finance is meant to provide the foundation for the understanding of finance, but basic concepts are taken for granted. This unstable foundation leads to the paradox of budding investors finishing their lengthy formal education programmes who are still unaware of basic finance and economic concepts.

In his introduction to 'The Education of a Value Investor', Guy Spier writes 'My goal in writing this book is to share some of what I've learned on my path as an investor …' (p. 1). Spier's education was what many ambitious young investors' dreams are made of: Politics, Philosophy and Economics at Oxford University (First Class degree) and an MBA at Harvard Business School. One might expect that Guy already knew all he needed about investing the day he set his foot outside HBS. Whilst Guy is clear that his education provided a firm footing, his 'investor education' was actually the result of an adventurous (perilous) journey based on 'experience'. In fact there is an entire chapter dedicated to the 'The Perils of Elite Education'.

Democratisation and specialisation

Some of the inadequacies of our education system could be the result of specialisation from increasing democratisation of investment.

Reamer and Downing ('Investment, a History', 2016) analyse the history of investment over the centuries and argue the process of democratisation of investment—the extension of investment activities access to the broader population—was the result of the industrial revolution, the advent of joint-stock companies and the development of public markets.[3]

---

3. In the early days of commerce there was no separation between the roles of business owners and managers. Both of these functions were typically performed by a single person (the owner/ manager). With economic advancement and the establishment of property rights, it became possible to grow businesses and operate them at scale that was beyond the capacity of the owner/ manager. The concepts of partnerships and joint-stock companies were born. It became possible to own parts of businesses, even multiple businesses without taking part in the management of operations. This crystalised the separation between ownership and control. This is a fundamental moment in the world of investment. It provided the basis for investing in equities but also for speculative behaviour. With the creation of public markets it became possible for investors to exchange ownership. This gave them the ability to become owners of businesses for periods shorter than the economic life of the underlying physical assets. This had a number of implications for (1) types of investors and (2) market dynamics.

As a result of more fluid ownership, financial markets grew more complex. The days when interested parties would meet to negotiate the price of shares before buying and selling them are long gone. Now there are well-organised exchanges where people can buy and sell their shares. Instead of owning shares in a few carefully selected businesses, people can now invest in tracker funds that give them exposure to a broad basket of stocks. As markets have evolved, the relation between the buyer and seller and the underlying has largely been lost. You are probably a part owner of a significant number of stocks, but you may not even know their names, much less their activities. The separation between ownership and management—specialisation—is a key feature of our society. You might put some money away for your pension but you do not have the time to buy a company to produce a return on capital, so you delegate the process to someone else. You buy a financial asset with a view of getting a financial return.

The net effect of democratisation and specialisation has been the proliferation in roles. Exchange takes place within an official equity market, with stock traders, market makers and broker dealers amongst the parties involved. The company is normally assisted by a broker who helps it with the pricing of shares and investment opportunities. The shareholder is normally assisted by a financial advisor, but she may decide to delegate her investment decisions to an asset or a wealth manager. Equities may creep into your portfolios in many other different ways, as part of a life insurance policy or as part of your pension investment. Each is subject to its own regulators and legal frameworks. You then have various service providers to each party, consultants, lawyers, auditors, accounting firms, financial analysts and the media.

The investment muddle

We have come a long way in democratising investments. Buying and selling shares has become far easier and transaction costs are minimal. Several platforms make investing easy, in theory. Information about investment opportunities is available like never before, greatly facilitated by the Internet. These advances have indeed made investing a more democratic process. *We are certainly better off than we were, but we are almost certainly more confused.* You may own equities, either directly (single stocks) or indirectly (through your pension fund). Specialised reviews and TV channels talk only about equities and equity markets. Most newspapers have a section dedicated to financial markets. However, ask several people simple questions such as 'What is a share? How do you value a company such as Amazon? What drives equity prices? What is your long term expected rate of return on equities?' and chances are you will get some very different answers.[4]

Digging further into a specific subject may not bring you much clarification. Take valuation. Aswath Damodaran is a world-renowned expert in the field and has written many excellent books on the topic. Nevertheless he provides a good example of how excessive specialisation can end up failing society. In his *The Little Book of Valuation*, he has a section called 'some truths about valuation' (p. 7), there are two paragraphs titled (1) 'All valuations are biased' and (2) 'Most valuations (even good ones) are wrong'. It appears that, in the search for the truth, we end up complicating things further.

The democratisation of investment is an important development of our capitalistic societies but the proliferation of stakeholders, intermediaries and participants adds complexity and distracts people from the basics of the investment process. *The net effect is a muddle where people do not understand what equities represent, what matters and what does not and how they ought to address fundamental issues.*

Fundamental analysis as a way forward

Such muddle means that we end up failing investors both at the micro and at the macro level.

At a micro level, such confusion possibly explains why so many people are resorting to passive investments. In a chaotic world, you either take control or look for the simplest approach at the lowest cost. The significant growth in passive investing would suggest that the battle is lost. I think space for a true investment process will always exist and the more popular passive investing becomes, the more important it will be to have a strong investment process based on a sound valuation framework.

At a macro level, there is no debate about the role of equities in our economies. Still, equities is capital and play a fundamental role in our society. The continuous retrenchment of government from providing a secure pension for retirement in several western countries means that consumers must develop a better understanding of equities, valuation and investment.

---

4. If you are looking for evidence, ask your family and friends which of the following two statements more accurately describes equity markets: (1) equity markets are a casino: you can make and lose a lot of money and the markets are full of speculators; (2) equity markets offer opportunities for exchanging ownership of real companies and a place where investors provide capital with a view of gaining a reasonable return in the long term. One might assume a significant number of respondents would describe equity markets as a casino because one would not expect the average person understand the real nature of equity markets, that is a place for exchange ownership of companies. Still, even more troublesome is that if you were to ask a similar question to some experts in the field you would probably have similar divergent views, a phenomenon best highlighted by Spier in his book.

The world of equities is complex, but it does not need to be. Investment is about capital and return; a capitalistic system is about capital and return, equities is about capital and return. The democratisation of investment requires a sound understanding of capital and return, but for this we must start from first principles and ensure that what we measure is done in a correct manner.

This is the frame of mind that I had when writing this book. The focus is on capital and return from an equity investors' perspective, but the discussion aims to promote a broader debate and research on equities, both at the macro and at the micro level. Passing more responsibilities to the end consumer requires both more research on equities and better education. This is particularly important at a time where there is little return on many asset classes. It also matters as the negative impact of past investments on the environment are evident. There is much talk in equities of environmental, social and governance investing. This is not a fad, it is the inevitable side-effect of the democratisation of investments. Addressing such issues in an intelligent manner does require a proper understanding of equities, valuation and investment, which I hope this book will address.

Chapter 1

Investment and valuation

The task of art today is to bring chaos into order.

Theodor Adorno

Chapter Outline

The challenge of the real equity investors

Investing is challenging in any asset class, particularly for equities. Investors in fixed income have all the necessary information: price, valuation (the yield), the maturity of the bond and the credit rating of the issuer. For equity investors, there is certainly an abundance of information from brokers, the Internet and the media, but it is often difficult to make sense of such information.

At a fundamental level, the primary information includes the share price and the earnings released by companies, which provide the basis for multiple valuation metrics (dividend yield, free cash flow yield, EV/EBITDA, price-to-earnings ratio and price-to-book ratio), but investors tend to be unclear about which metric ought to be used and why. Additional complexity comes from (1) the absence of maturity for the investment unlike credit (the decision of when to sell is left with the investor), (2) the lack of a metric rating the quality of the asset (unlike credit) and (3) the investor's need to choose between receiving a return in price or dividends (the first being very volatile and the second more stable, but with a permanent risk that it may be cut in the future). The challenge is even greater when one considers that prices

Valuing and Investing in Equities. DOI: https://doi.org/10.1016/B978-0-12-813848-9.00001-7

1

are driven by two factors that can mutate over time, that is earnings and the discount rate.

Imagine instead a situation where you have an understanding of the valuation, how the business to which you are providing capital is financed (by debt holders or other providers of financial capital, such as pension and financial lessors), the capital invested in the business, the operational return the company generates on its business, and its true level of profitability. There is still uncertainty but this information would provide you with a sound basis for investment decisions. This is the nirvana of the real investor. Utopia? Not in my opinion. The secret is to focus on fundamentals and to think that when you are buying equities, you ought to run a process similar to when you are buying a company with your own money. Framing the process in such a manner has implications for (1) the time frame of the investment, (2) how one deals with noise from media and analysts and (3) your own analysis of share price dynamics.

I will share with the reader what a 'real investment process' looks like, by starting from first principles: capital and return.

The fundamentals of equities investing: capital and returns

The fundamental pillars of an investment process are capital and return. These core elements are valid for any kind of investment. In the world of equities, you find a separation between those providing capital, that is the investors (broadly defined as anyone providing financial capital) and those needing it (companies). Investors provide capital to companies and expect to be compensated by a return. Companies deploy financial capital in their operations, which will generate a return, used ultimately to reward the owners of financial capital.

The relationship between the investors and management is straightforward: the provision of financial capital is the monetary basis supporting the business. The company uses the financial capital in the business to invest in operations, stores, plants and machinery. The proceeds generate an operational return, which is used to reward the investor with a financial return that compensates for the risk taken. At a practical level, some of the financial return is distributed through dividends and some is retained by the business. The process can be simplified in the following manner (Fig. 1.1):

1. The investor, who provides financial capital.
2. The company that uses the financial capital and employs it in a business.
3. The business generates an operational return.
4. The operational return is the basis for providing the investor with a financial return, part of which is paid to the provider of financial capital and part reinvested in the business.

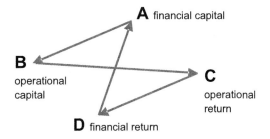

FIGURE 1.1   Capital and return.

This typology will be used throughout the book as I like to consider capital and return from the two different perspectives, the investor and the company. Thinking of a coin is a simple and effective way to think of the investment process. On one side, there are the financial investors and their return expectations, and management on the other, deploying capital to generate a return.

The duality of the investment process was formalised in the 15th century by a Franciscan friar, Luca Pacioli, in a book *Summa de arithmetica, geometria. proportioni et proportionalita* (1494), where he presented the system used by the merchants in Venice for the book-keeping of their investments. The system was the basis for the development of the current double-entry accounting system, which displays the operating assets on one side and the financial liabilities on the other.

> Tenet #1 of our investment framework: the starting point of an investment process ought to be the balance sheet, the analysis of the assets and liabilities, which is normally defined as the 'stock'.

When buying a piece of a company you must look at its assets. Too often this does not happen; instead, the focus of much analysis is on earnings and earnings dynamics, which is normally defined as the 'flow'. Earnings are important because they are the combination of the capital and returns (Earnings = Capital × Return). They compensate the owner for providing capital at risk, but earnings on their own make little sense. An example may help. A few years back there was a lot of noise about the outrageous amount of earnings generated by the Energy sector. Stories about outsized earnings were making the front pages of newspapers around the world. The profits were high but nevertheless normal when compared with the amount of capital invested in those businesses. Energy in 2010 made 260bn USD in Economic Earnings with 4100bn on net capital, a cash return of 6.4%.

What was more outrageous was the economic earnings made in the Consumer Staples sector, which were 178bn with 1500bn on net capital, a cash return of 11.9%. There were over three times more capital invested in Energy than in Consumer Staples. Still, a mere 50% more earnings was enough to call for the nationalisation of the industry. Comparing capital and earnings would have certainly led to a more balanced conversation.

The two sides of the investment process in an equation

The best way to summarise the investment process is by the investment equation (Fig. 1.2). On one side, you have the investor and their financial capital with an expected rate of return; on the other side, you have the company with its operational capital generating a return. The value of the two components can diverge, but ultimately there has to be a match between what the company is able to produce and what the investor can expect.

$$\text{Fin. Capital } (A) \times \text{Fin. Return } (B) = \text{Op. Capital } (C) \times \text{Op. Return } (D)$$

FIGURE 1.2   The investment equation.

Tenet #2 of our investment framework: (1) investment is about equation in Fig 1.2 and (2) fundamental valuation is about the analysis of the components of the equation.

The many names associated with the components of the investment equation

The components of the investment equation have historically been labelled in several different ways:

1. *Financial Capital* (or *Price* or *Enterprise Value* or *Market Cap*) is the value of the financial capital associated with the company. Various names may be associated with different components of the total financial capital associated with a business.
2. *Financial Return* (or *Expected Rate of Return* or *Discount Rate* or *Cost of Capital*) is the rate of return that financial investors expect when they risk their capital.[1] The essential point is that the rate of return for a financial investor is, for a manager, the benchmark against which to measure

---

1. I subscribe to the view that there is a difference between the cost of debt and cost of equity in the medium term (Modigliani and Miller, 1958). The financial return includes (1) the dividend and (2) the difference between the price paid and price received.

investment decisions (i.e. the cost of capital). This is also defined as the discount rate, that is the rate at which earnings tend to be discounted to define the fair price. Hence the expected rate of return is equivalent to the cost of capital.[2]

3. *Operational Capital* (or *Capital Invested*, or *Capital Employed* or *Equity* or *Book or Net Capital Invested*) defines how much capital is actually employed in the business.

4. *Operational Return* [or *Return on Equity (RoE)*, or *Return on Capital Invested* or *Return on Capital Employed* or *Cash Return on Capital Invested*] represents the return on the operational capital invested in the business. The concept of return on equity is concerned more with the liability side of the balance sheet, whereas the other metrics concentrate on the asset side.

The many ways of presenting the investment equation

The investment equation (Fig. 1.2) has been presented in many different guises and under different names. They are often seen as different valuation ratios, but they are a rearrangement of the same equation. In this section, I present the various ways of presenting the investment equation. Each of us may have a favourite, but it is essential to appreciate that they all derive from the same equation expressed in Fig. 1.2.

$$\frac{\text{Price}}{\text{Book}} = \frac{\text{RoE}}{\text{Cost of capital}} \quad \text{or} \quad \frac{(A)}{(C)} = \frac{(D)}{(B)} \tag{1.1}$$

The price-to-book is a function of the return on capital given a discount rate. If you are buying a company, then it makes sense to look at the price of the actual book (capital) operationally invested in the business. By rearranging the investment equation, you get to look at an investment through the price-to-book approach. The analysis is straightforward: given a discount rate of 5% and an RoE of 10%, an investment ought to trade on a price-to-book ratio of 2× to be fairly valued. If the expected rate of return is 5% and the RoE 5%, the price-to-book ratio ought to be 1×. This way of presenting the investment equation helps in abnormal situations, such as booms and busts when the RoE may either be too high or too low. Investors, by normalising the RoE, are able to estimate the correct price to attach to the book.

$$\text{Price} = \frac{\text{Earnings (RoE} \times \text{Book)}}{\text{Discount rate}} \quad \text{or} \quad (A) = \frac{(C \times D)}{(B)} \tag{1.2}$$

The price of a company is the value of its discounted future earnings, with earnings being the result of return and capital. This is the formula that

2. The absolute level of the discount rate and changes in the discount rate have a fundamental role on the level of equity markets and its dynamics as well as on the economy. This is something that I will explore in detail in Chapter 4, Stock picking based on economic fundamentals.

most will recognise: the price of an asset is a function of the discounted value of the earnings. A company with a RoE of 10% and a book of 100 will generate earnings of 10. If the company can generate these earnings into perpetuity and I discount them at 5%, the fair price for the investment is 200. However, earnings are not constant and need to be modelled, but they are difficult to forecast (see Chapter 4: Stock picking based on economic fundamentals).

$$\frac{P}{E} \text{ ratio} = \frac{1}{\text{Disc. rate}} \quad \text{or} \quad \frac{(A)}{(C \times D)} = \frac{1}{(B)} \qquad (1.3)$$

$$\frac{E}{P} \text{ (Earnings yield)} = \text{Disc. rate} \quad \text{or} \quad \frac{(C \times D)}{(A)} = (B) \qquad (1.4)$$

$$\text{Disc. rate} = \text{Earn.s yield or the inverse of } \frac{P}{E} \text{ or } (B) = \frac{(C \times D)}{(A)} \qquad (1.5)$$

The previous three formulae present three different ways to relate valuation to the discount rate, as there is a direct relation between the discount rate and the earnings multiple. A company with a price of 200 and earnings of 10 will be on a PE ratio on $20 \times$. This is possibly the most frequently used part of any financial analysis and, for many, will define whether a stock is attractive or not. If they assume that the company can maintain the same capital and return to perpetuity, investors will also look at the inverse, the earnings yield, which tells us what the investor can expect under certain assumptions—in this case 5%. This is a useful ratio when comparing equities to other yielding assets. The third interpretation is less frequently used, but there is a direct relation between the discount rate and valuation ratios. The discount rate (the expected rate of return or cost of capital) is the inverse of the *P/E* ratio, or the earnings yield.

The dark and the bright sides of valuation and how they drive price changes

The entire valuation framework for investing in equities, and its derivative ratios, is built around the initial investment equation in Fig. 1.2 but, even so, applying it can be challenging. The reader will soon see the ensuing complexities, as three of the four factors in the investment equation can drive changes in the share price. This is highly confusing, especially for fixed income investors whose coupon hardly ever changes. Equity investors, instead, must deal with changes in (1) earnings and their drivers (capital and return) and (2) the discount rate.

Tenet #3 of our investment framework: changes in price can be driven by changes in (1) the discount rate and (2) capital and returns.

Investors ought to develop a proper understanding of how each change affects prices. I will cover these issues more in detail in Chapter 4, Stock picking based on economic fundamentals. Investors normally focus on analysing what I define as the bright side of the investment equation, that is earnings and their drivers (capital and return), but they should also understand the effect of changes in the dark side of valuation (the discount rate) as those changes have a fundamental impact on prices. I call it the dark side, as it is often ignored, but is nonetheless relevant. An example should help (Fig. 1.3). Suppose there is company with a constant level of earnings and capital, but as a result of an external event (earthquake, financial crisis and terrorism) there is a significant increase in risk aversion and investors demand a higher rate of return to provide capital at risk. In this example, the discount rate goes from 5% to 10%. Nothing has changed with regard to the company but the price of the company has halved. This adjustment in valuation is necessary to maintain the equilibria because if operating capital and operating return are constant, then the price (A) becomes a function of the discount rate (D).

	Stage 1	Stage 2
Discount rate	5%	10%
RoE	20%	20%
Capital invested	1000	1000
Price =	(20%×1000)/5% = **4000**	(20%×1000)/10% = **2000**

FIGURE 1.3 How changes in the discount rate affect price.

The example is exaggerated, but a 1% change in the expected rate of return (6% instead of 5%), would still have an impact of 666 or 17%! The opposite is true when the expected rate of return goes down.

Tenet #4 of our investing framework: an investor should never ignore the impact that changes in the discount rate have on the price of equities.

Equity research analysts struggle with such changes and normally ignore them, but as an example, nearly four-fifths of the 49% fall in equity markets between December 2007 and March 2009 (CROCI Talk, 10 March 2009, Counting the cost) was driven by changes in risk appetite, driving investors to demand a higher expected rate of return. The remaining 9% was a function of a possible lower level of earnings going forward. Changes in risk appetite are important but not well understood.

Modelling earnings into perpetuity and the relative challenges

I have thus far presented a simplistic model with earnings assumed to be constant to perpetuity. Reality is more complex and will be analysed in Chapter 4, Stock picking based on economic fundamentals, in greater detail. Equity analysts try to forecast the future dynamics of earnings. The simple investment equation then becomes:

$$P = E(y_1) + E(y_2) + \cdots + E(y_n) + \cdots \quad \text{discounted to today's value}$$

However, forecasting that far into the future is an art rather than a science. The analysis is necessarily speculative, something I investigate in Chapter 4, Stock picking based on economic fundamentals.

Section 1

CROCI on valuation

Why valuation is so important for investor

Tenet #5 of our investment process: the investor's choice of valuation process is a function of her position in our typology (see the Introduction for a review). The closer the investor is to number 1, the more she focuses on valuation:

Where would you put yourself?

Where would you put yourself?

	1	2	3	4	5
Investor					*Speculator*

If you are the Real Investor (typology one), you tend to be sceptical in nature. When you see a phenomenal deal in front of you, the first question you ask is 'value or value trap'? There are two types of value traps. The first type relates to a due diligence process on the accounts. Think of buying a house that costs $10m and that you could rent out for $1m per year in return. It may look like an amazing deal as the rental yield seems to be 10%, but then you find in the notes that this is only valid for the first year and from year 2 you need to share 95% of the rent with the landowner ... What may look like an amazing deal is clearly a value trap. The second type of value traps refers to a business that is not sustainable in the long term. Think of the same house being on a sea cliff in a region subject to sea erosion. In five years the house will be gone and all you will have recouped is the rent for 5 years ($5m).

There are three chapters in this section. Chapter 2, Valuing nonfinancial companies, focuses on the due diligence process on nonfinancial companies; Chapter 3, The analytical idiosyncrasies of banks, focuses on banks. This is our heritage. CROCI is, in the strictest sense, a due diligence process that concentrates on assessing the true economic value of capital, return and of the price paid. Our approach is comparable to what a private investor would do if she was thinking of buying the company with her own money. This process is run by the CROCI analysts. There are 10 senior CROCI analysts supported by close to 35 people conducting due diligence on nearly 1000 stocks, representing 85% of the weight of the major global indices. The process ensures that there are no differences in due diligence across sectors and markets so that the results are fully comparable. The CROCI analysts are industry experts. They have a complete understanding of the economics of business, capital, return and valuation, but they do not make recommendations. There is no obligation to cover a stock if it fails the due diligence process. You cannot think of buying something where you have significant concerns about disclosure.

In Chapter 4, Stock picking based on economic fundamentals, I refine the valuation framework. The due diligence on accounts is a necessary first step, but how do we judge whether a company is attractive or expensive on valuation? This chapter provides a fundamental introduction to next section. The fair share price of a stock is the net present value of its future earnings. Forecasting the future should thus be the primary objective of an investor. Still, fundamental variables are unknown (life and earnings profile) and a significant part of the valuation relates to events that might occur in the future. This makes forecasting an art rather than a science. The reader also needs to consider that the fair share price is influenced by a variable beyond the control of either management or analysts: the discount rate (the dark side). Brokers and research analysts focus on the short term, assuming that it is possible to extrapolate future events from the present. Our view is that investors in equities deserve an extra reward because they face structural uncertainty with regard to the outcome of the investment process and that much of the forecasting will not help. I instead suggest an approach in which the investor is aware of the scenario embedded in the share price. I run a fundamental analysis that aids the investor in assessing the attractiveness of the stock.

By the end of Chapter 4, Stock picking based on economic fundamentals, the reader will have a sound understanding of the CROCI approach to equities, valuation, the variables affecting price and its dynamics. The reader will also be able to analyse different scenarios for stocks. The next section covers the ways we use CROCI as a basis for an investment process.

Chapter 2

Valuing non-financial companies

Chapter Outline

The first step of an investment process is to decide which valuation ratio to use. Various valuation ratios can be derived out of information available in the accounts [price-to-book, dividend yield (DY), price-to-earnings ratio and price-to-cash earnings (P/CE)]. The most frequently used valuation ratio is the price-to-earnings ratio. It is certainly the most comprehensive. DY does not provide information about the profits a company actually generates, but what it distributes. The price-to-book ratio provides information about the price of the equity capital but not about the return generated by the equity. The advantage of the *P/E* ratio is that it brings together the price paid and the earnings that are meant to be received and it can also be seen as the relationship between the price paid on the capital and the return generated by the capital or [price-to-book ratio (*P/B*)]/RoE. Its inverse, the earnings yield, provides investors information about the expected rate of return on equities if earnings are stable in perpetuity. As Robin Wensley (my PhD supervisor) used to say, *there is beauty in simplicity* and I would argue that the *P/E* is simply beautiful when properly measured. Once the ratio to use is defined,

Valuing and Investing in Equities. DOI: https://doi.org/10.1016/B978-0-12-813848-9.00002-9
11

the investor can start to look for attractively priced stocks, but the first question that ought to come to our mind is 'value or value trap'?

The price-to-earnings ratio: what you see is not what you get

Back in 2014 I gave a presentation at a press event where the objective was show why CROCI made a difference. I have used that set of data ever since. Fig. 2.1 shows the *P/E* ratio of 10 well-known listed companies in 2014. For each company there are two ratios: the first on the left uses publically available information, that is listed price and stated earnings, and the ratio on the right shows valuation after our due diligence process on the accounts. The relative ranking is in brackets.

There are small valuation differences in some cases (LVMH, Apple and Amgen), but differences can be substantial in other cases (Amazon,

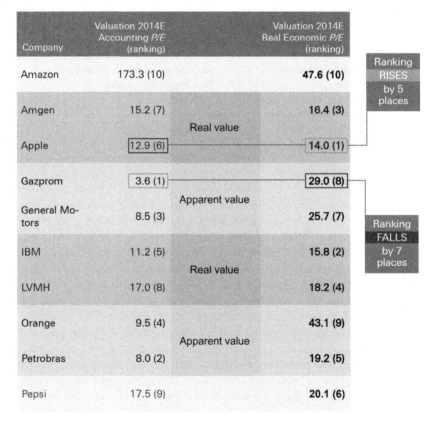

FIGURE 2.1 The valuation of 10 stocks using stated and adjusted numbers. *Data from DWS and CROCI.*

Gazprom, GM and Orange). How can there be such significant differences in valuation? And why? The reason is simple. Accounts are not prepared with equity investors in mind. They are prepared to meet regulatory accounting standards defined by the accounting profession and conform to a country's regulatory policies. We adjust those accounts to serve real investors, those thinking that in buying equities they are buying companies with their own money. The difference in valuation is thus the result of applying a due diligence process that establishes the real economic value of the company.

Tenet #6 of our investment process: always be sceptical of accounting valuation ratios, as what you see is not necessarily what you get.

I will provide a few examples to highlight this point. Did you know that banks prepare different sets of accounts, one standard set of accounts for investors and another for regulators? Which should you use? Or that some companies listed in the United States and in Europe may file accounts using different accounting standards (US GAAP and IAS) with different levels of profits and assets? Were you aware that the same aircraft may have different depreciation schedules according to who owns it, which might have nothing to do with actual economic usage? Or that energy and mining companies may account for exploration costs in different ways? The point is simple: an investor may wish to compare valuation of companies across regions and sectors, but this is not possible without making adjustments to the price, to the assets and to the profitability of the company.

Some adjustments must be made to both price and earnings to ensure that the ratio reflects the true value of the company as measure by the P/E ratio.

$$\text{Company } \frac{P}{E} \text{ ratio} = \frac{\text{Mkt Cap } + \text{Adj.}}{\text{Earnings} + \text{Adj.}} = \frac{\text{Real Price}}{\text{Real Earnings}}$$

Once those adjustments are made, the relative ranking changes. The new ranking reflects what a real investor would achieve after deep due diligence on the accounts without taking a view of the long-term fortune of the business. We now have a sound basis for investment decisions.

The shortfalls of accounting valuation are well known, or are they?

The difference in ranking (Fig. 2.1) may come as a surprise to some given the wide use of international accounting standards, but equity investors have known about this problem for a long time. Progress has been made towards improving accounting standards to enable comparability, but challenges remain. Investors have tried to overcome the 'measurement' problem in several ways. Some use multiple financial ratios, whereas others use concepts such as risk premia to justify systematic differences in valuation. Unfortunately accounting measures are still widely used both in academia and in defining investment processes, which adds to the confusion. The net result is a compromise where investors buy value-driven financial products in the belief that they have genuine exposure to value, when this is rarely the case.

The invisible hand at work in valuation

The reality is that *equity investors are smarter than economists give them credit for, as they adjust prices to reflect the true level of valuation.* Take an investor who is looking for companies with a *P/E* ratio of $<20\times$. For a company with earnings of 10, the price ought to be 200. However, if the investor is aware that she can only get her hands on 50% of the stated profits, that is 5, then the fair price is 100 and she is correct in putting a multiple of $20\times$ on the 5, that is what she will receive. In other words, the stock trades on a real *P/E* ratio of $20\times$, even though its 'official' accounting *P/E* ratio is $10\times$! *There is value, based on accounting ratios, but it is optical rather than real.* The invisible hand has been at work, with the market adjusting for distortions. This issue is addressed in detail in Section 2, but the two charts show that this is effectively what happens. Fig. 2.2 shows the correlation between the two drivers of *P/E* (*P/B* and RoE) using accounting data; Fig. 2.3 shows the same correlation using CROCI data. The increase in correlation is strong evidence that the market looks at companies in a similar manner to us after making our adjustments!

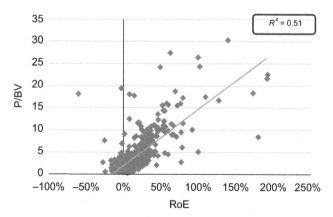

FIGURE 2.2 Correlation between P/BV and RoE. *Data from DWS and CROCI.*

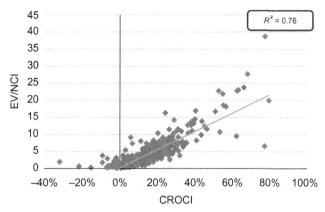

FIGURE 2.3   Correlation between EV/NCI and CROCI. *Data from DWS and CROCI.*

Two wrongs do not make one right: risk premia and EV/EBITDA

Our view is that the simplest way to rectify the problems created by accounting standards is to adjust the accounting distortions at the source. There is enough money in the world of finance to be vocal about the matter and to demand a set of accounting standards that properly serves equity investors. Instead, though, I have seen decades of analysis using flawed accounting data for investment processes. Academics have used accounting data as the basis for various hypotheses and have developed concepts of sector and market risk premia to justify differences in valuation ratios. Practitioners recognise the problems that accounting data bring and have sought refuge in supposedly cleaner valuation ratios such as EV/EVITDA. Both make the same mistake, trying to use two wrongs (risk premia plus wrong ratio) to get to the right valuation ratio.

Sector and country risk premia

Risk premia is a sound concept, but it should not be used in situations where it is conceptually not applicable. Risk premia is about an additional return versus another investment because of additional risk being taken. For example you would expect a junk bond to trade at a higher level than a triple-A rated bond. This difference is its risk premium. But when there is no underlying difference in risk between two investments, then risk premium has no place! Academic and practitioners have been guilty of using the concept of risk premia to justify differences in valuation between sectors and regions that are just not there in reality. The demonstration is in our correlation chart, you would not get a 0.76 correlation if such risk premia were genuinely present.

Why EV/EBITDA is just plain wrong as a valuation ratio

Enterprise Value (EV)/Earnings before Interest, Tax, Depreciation and Amortisation (EBITDA) is one of the most common and supposedly cleanest valuation ratios but is a wrong valuation ratio and should never be used even to compare valuations within the same sector. The ratio compares the EV (the sum of all financial liabilities, i.e. equity and debt), with the EBITDA. The underlying assumption is that EBITDA is a good proxy to the cash received before investments are made. However, (1) in the pharma sector and other sectors, the ratio is post-R&D expenditure, which is the real capex in the sector and ought to be excluded from the calculation of EBITDA; (2) tax rates may differ across companies and (3) EV/EBITDA delivers the wrong conclusions when two companies operate within the same sector but have different capital intensities.

Take two companies with very different capital/labour mixes (key accounting figures in bold). Company A spends more on labour than capital. Each year the company invests 10,000 in capital and depreciates 10,000 (average life 10 years). Company B spends more on capital than labour. Each year it spends 22,500 in capital and depreciates 22,500 (average life 5 years). The two investments have the same net income (5000), the same RoE and the same net capital. They are on the same valuation (as they ought to be) using an appropriate ratio, such as the *P/E* ratio. But using the EV/EBITDA ratio the conclusion would be that company B was more attractive than company A. This is wrong as the investments are equivalent!

	Company A	Company B
Enterprise value/price (no debt)	100,000	100,000
Capital (equity)	45,000	45,000
Return on capital (equity)	11.1%	11.1%
Sales	**50,000**	**50,000**
Operating costs	(x) 30,000	(x_1) 17,500
EBITDA	**20,000**	**32,500**
Depreciation	(y) 10,000	(y_1) 22,500
Pretax	**10,000**	**10,000**
Tax 50%	5000	5000
Net income	**5000**	**5000**
Price-to-earnings ratio	**20×**	**20×**
EV/EBITDA ratio	**5.0×**	**3.0×**

Other valuation ratios are not the solution for real investors

Practitioners, on the other hand, are aware of the problems embedded in accounting standards and have used multiple ratios to validate their analyses. If a company is cheap on *P/E*, they will seek confirmation by looking at multiple ratios (DY, P/CE, EV to free cash flow, EV to earnings before interests after tax, EV to earnings before interests and tax and the *P/B*). It is beyond the scope of this book to do a literature review of the virtues and shortcoming of each ratio, but measurement problems are best addressed by creating a sound basis for valuation rather than by inventing inferior measures.

How using accounting data also creates problems for portfolio construction

The problem with using accounting data as a basis for investment is magnified when stock selection is brought into portfolio construction. The primary role of traditional equity portfolio managers ought to be the selection of the most attractive stocks. However, it is not easy to compare valuations across sectors and countries with accounting data. The result is that investors often resort to selecting the most attractive stocks within a sector or region under the assumption that valuation will be comparable within the same region and the same sector. This approach brings other problems, though. First, sector definitions can be flawed (Is a car maker comparable to an hotelier or a retailer? Why is an airliner an Industrial stock?). Second, the inability to compare valuations across sectors and markets means investors focus on macro factors to define sector and region weights. Stock picking thus becomes a jumble of top-down and bottom-up analysis. This would not happen if the stock picker has a sound framework enabling full comparability of valuations across sectors and countries.

> Tenet #7 of our investment framework: the true comparable feature of companies is not their sector or region, but rather their capital and returns.

Gazprom: why valuation was not attractive after it was adjusted

The analysis of the adjustments necessary to Gazprom's accounts provides a good introduction to the broader topic of adjustments that can yield a sound basis for investing in equities (Fig. 2.4).

In 2013 Gazprom generated revenues of 4970bn RUB. Gazprom operates in a capital intensive industry producing and transporting gas. The assets used by the company tend to have a long economic life on average, around 30 years, which in a mature company will lead to the same assets having an average age of 15 years. To estimate the correct level of profitability, one needs compare the level of revenues generated in a specific year with the capital invested in the money of that same year. At the same time, net profits ought to be calculated after subtracting a charge for the consumption of physical capital as measured in the same year when revenues were produced. This is a necessary adjustment to compare (1) valuations with companies operating in the same market but that have different ages, (2) valuations across different economies with different inflation rates and (3) valuations of the same company over different periods if inflation has changed.

Gazprom	Reported	Real
Net tangible assets	9,600	**24,126**
Equity	10,050	25,854
Revenues	4,970	4,970
Depreciation	425	**1,216**
Net profits	884	**160**
Mkt cap/enterprise value	3,163	**4,651**
P/E ratio	3.6x	29.0x

FIGURE 2.4 Gazprom − selected data − 2013 annual report. *Data from DWS, CROCI and company accounts.*

In Russia inflation was high in the decade before 2013. Adjusting the assets for inflation brought Gazprom's 2003 value from 9600bn RUB to 24,126bn RUB (i.e. 2.5 × what was recorded), the real value of depreciation went from 425bn RUB to 1216bn RUB and the real level of profits came down from 884bn RUB to 160bn RUB.

The other important adjustment was to the price. The equity value was 3163bn RUB, but adding other financial liabilities increased the value to a real price of 4651bn RUB. As a comparison must be made on a like-for-like basis, any charge related to those financial liabilities would have been removed from the cost base to compare the real level of profits with all the financial liabilities. The net effect of the various adjustments was a real economic *P/E* ratio of 29.0 $\times$, far off the 3.6 $\times$ value estimated using stated accounts.

How inflation distorts accounts

The following example shows the case of the same company operating in two countries with different inflation rates. In both cases we are dealing with a company with an average asset life of 30 years and investing 1000 of 'real' capital. The difference is that in the first case, there is no inflation and in the second case, inflation is running at a constant value of 10%. The examples show the accounts for the two companies after 30 years.

	No inflation, year 30	With inflation, year 30 (not adjusted)	Real values, year 30 adjusted
Investment	1000	15,863	15,863
Gross capital invested	30,000	164,494	475,893
Accumulated depreciation	15,500	50,314	245,878
Net capital invested	14,500	114,180	230,015
Depreciation charge	1000 (real)	5483 (accounting)	15,863 (real)
Life (years)	30 (30,000/1000)	30 (164,494/5483)	30 (475,893/15,863)
Age (years)	15.5 (15,500/1000)	9.2 (50,314/5483)	15.5 (245,878/15,863)

The example shows how in a country with inflation, the level of profits will be artificially boosted. While the company appears to be spending 3 $\times$ what it is depreciating, the 'real' level of capital spent is the same as it is consuming. To assess the amount of capital effectively consumed to generate revenues, the depreciation charge would need to increase to maintenance capex (i.e. 15,863), which would negatively impact profits. The same process must be applied to the assets. It appears that the gross capital is 164,494, but the real capital is closer to be 15,863 $\times$ 30 = 475,893.

The distortion that inflation brings to accounts and valuation is analysed in detail in Chapter 9, Equities, inflation and valuation.

Nothing new – Coca Cola and Exxon in the 1980s

The sceptical reader may argue that if this adjustment was ever this relevant, it would have been addressed. In fact, adjusting the accounts for inflation became an important matter in the 1980s, when regulators required companies to publish both GAAP and inflation-adjusted financial statements. *[The US Financial Accounting Standards Board] believes that users' understanding of the past performance of an enterprise and their ability to assess future cash flows will be severely limited until [inflation adjusted accounts are] included in financial reports* (FAS33, Financial Accounting Standards Board, September 1979). Companies thereafter started to publish notes to their accounts highlighting the impact of inflation. Here are two illustrative examples taken from the 1982 annual reports of two well-known corporations (Figs. 2.5 and 2.6).

	As reported ($m)	Adjusted for inflation ($m)
Sales	103,559	103,559
Depreciation	**3,333**	**5,929**
Net income	4,186	−296
Equity	28,440	69,154
ROE	14.7%	NM
Dividend yield	10.5%	10.5%
P/E ratio*	**6.0x**	**NM**

FIGURE 2.5 Exxon: selected data 1982 annual report. *Data from DWS, CROCI and company accounts. Note (*): Appendix to Chapter 9, Equities, inflation and valuation, has more details on Exxon. The estimation to the devaluation of the financial debt, which would have had a marginal positive effect on profitability and put the stock on a P/E of 200 ×.*

	As reported ($m)	Adjusted for inflation ($m)
Sales	6,250	6,250
Depreciation	149	215
Net income	512	408
Equity	2,779	3,617
ROE	18.4%	11.2%
Dividend yield	6.6%	6.6%
P/E ratio	**9.4x**	**11.9x**

FIGURE 2.6 Coca Cola: selected data 1982 annual report. *Data from DWS, CROCI and company accounts.*

On the basis of what was reported, Exxon appeared very attractively valued in contrast to Coca Cola. It had a marginally lower RoE but it had close to twice the DY and half the level of valuation based on *P/E*. However, making the adjustments (which the company disclosed in their accounting notes), would suggest a different situation. Other examples are illustrated in appendix to Chapter 9, Equities, inflation and valuation.

Over the years, this practice of adding notes to the accounts to show the impact of inflation has been abandoned. There are two accounting standards, the historical cost accounted and the current cost accounted. The latter ought to be used, but rarely is. Today, it is still important to adjust for inflation as (1) a small amount of inflation on very long-lived assets still has a meaningful impact and (2) deflation may be an issue in certain countries. Adjusting for inflation is as important as adjusting for deflation. In a deflationary environment, the real level of profits will be higher than it appears and the real level of assets lower.

CROCI as a form of due diligence to assess the value of companies

The challenges facing investors are now becoming clear. It may not be easy to be sheltered from market noise and the world of speculation, but investors possess inadequate tools for their jobs. Academics and passive investors make the problem more difficult to solve through their use of flawed data for research and investments. The principles of book-keeping may have been created centuries ago to provide support to Venetian merchants, but they have taken on a life of their own, and the current system does not provide proper support to investment decisions. The evidence is that the adjustments made to Gazprom and to the other nine stocks have significant impacts on valuation. A real investor, one putting her own money at risk, would be a fool to use accounting measures, given that these 10 names are far from unique in needing adjustment.

When applying the CROCI methodology, there are four adjustments that ought to be made to the reported set of accounts to move from an accounting basis to an investment basis:

1. Include all financial assets and liabilities in estimating the value of a company and remove financial charges when estimating the real level of profitability.
2. Adjust for the distortions created by inflation
3. Account for hidden capital (intangible and off-balance sheet assets and liabilities).
4. Estimate the economic life of the assets correctly to estimate the correct rate of return on capital invested.

Adjustment one − revising the price for all financial liabilities. When valuing a company, an investor ought to look at all providers of financial capital. We thus add to market capitalisation all the various financial liabilities and move to an EV concept. This means that we consider all the financing sources of the business, anything that has a claim on profitability. Most of those sources are on the balance sheet, debt being the main one, but we also consider advance payments, warranties, deferred revenues, nuclear decommission liabilities and other financial provisions, some of which are off-balance sheet. It is also important to evaluate the values created by accountants when they considered liabilities. This has been the case for example for pension accounting, where both assets and liabilities are included and mixed with other items. A more detailed analysis is recommended, but it is beyond the scope of this book. Adding items to the balance sheet also impacts the P&L as it is necessary to estimate the level of profits that the company generates for all providers of financial capital.

Adjustment two − inflation. If you buy a company, the assets ought to be measured in current cost. This adjustment has already been highlighted in the cases of Gazprom, Coca Cola and Exxon. Assets are often measured in historical money. Investing is about the profit generated today on the capital expressed in today's money, and the level of profits must be estimated after a charge for the consumption of capital measured in today's money.

Adjustment three − hidden capital (leasing and intangibles). There are two forms of hidden capital: leasing and intangibles. *Leasing* relates to a financial arrangement with a third party to use an asset in exchange for a regular payment with an interest payment attached to it. Think of leasing a car: you enter a financial obligation and it affects your credit rating. Companies lease stores, trains, aeroplanes, ships and other assets. Rules related to operating leases have recently changed, but historically both assets and liabilities have been put off balance sheet. If you do not bring back both assets and liabilities, certain valuation ratios such as price-to-book will be distorted. The return on capital will also be higher when you move assets and liabilities off the balance sheet and comparability will be compromised. An adjustment must be made, which is important as the investor, the ultimate owner of the company, will take over the financial obligations related to such assets.

Adjusting for *intangibles* is more complex. The best approach to understanding the adjustment they require is to start from first principles: what is capital? How do you define it? Strictly speaking, *capital is about the ability to enjoy the benefit associated with an expenditure for multiple years.* If the benefit has an economic life that is less than a year, it is an operating cost; if the benefit is for longer than a year, then it is an investment that results in the formation of fixed capital. At a practical level, it is easy to think of *physical* capital: cars, plants, machinery. We see them and by observing the rate of deterioration in physical assets, we can estimate their lives. It is more difficult to do the same with *intangible* expenditures. Still, think of pharmaceutical companies or of companies with strong brand values such as L'Oreal, Procter & Gamble, Tiffany and LVMH. Both sets of companies have significant expenditures associated with creating economic benefits over multiple years. The revenues of a pharmaceutical company are associated with research made in the past, but no assets for research can be found in the accounting balance sheet. The reason is simple. Historically, accounting has been driven by the principle of *prudence*. If you cannot measure something precisely, write it off in the P&L; so R&D has been written off. Measuring how much of it and its economic life is not easy, but it is possible and most importantly this process takes place during a corporate acquisition. Within the box, I report about the acquisition of Pharmacia by Pfizer in 2003. The most important asset, R&D, was not on the balance sheet, but it appeared after the acquisition. In reality it was always there but was hidden.

The correct approach is to analyse what companies spend on R&D or marketing, assess whether those expenditures ought to be capitalised and over what period of time and make the relevant adjustments to the P&L and balance sheet.

A case study on capitalising R&D: Pfizer's acquisition of Pharmacia in 2003

Pfizer acquired Pharmacia for approximately $56 billion in 2003. Before the acquisition in December 2002, Pfizer had $10.7bn of tangible fixed assets and $0.9bn of intangible assets other than goodwill. The reported accounts of Pharmacia from the same period show $5.6bn of tangible fixed assets, $1.15bn of goodwill and $393m of intangible assets other than goodwill. On completion of this acquisition in April 2003, Pfizer recorded Pharmacia's assets and liabilities in their books at their respective fair values.

This revaluation of Pharmacia's assets and liabilities was expected to result in a restatement, but the scale was hard to anticipate. Intangible assets saw the biggest jump. Their value increased from the $393m that was reported in Pharmacia's books to $37.2bn. The largest component of these acquired intangibles was Developed Technology Rights, which were valued at $31.2bn.

These Developed Technology Rights represent the right to develop, use or sell the acquired products, compounds and intellectual property. These and similar assets are some of the most important assets of pharmaceutical companies, and future revenues and profits depend upon them. But they are not reported in

(Continued)

(Continued)

the financial statements in a consistent manner. The accounting treatment seems to suggest that these assets were created as a result of the acquisition. Of course, in reality these intangible assets existed before Pfizer acquired Pharmacia but were simply not reported on the latter's balance sheet.

Even the $31.2bn of Developed Technology Rights does not represent the entirety of Pharmacia's extant intangible assets. The recognised value only accounts for those assets whose development is sufficiently advanced. A further $5.0bn of such assets were disclosed as 'In Process Research & Development', all of which were written off as expenses in Pfizer's books.

For brand-owning companies, there is much information about brand creation and what is required to maintain it. There is a risk of confusion between brands and household names. Many energy stocks (BP, Exxon and Total) are household names, but we attach no value to the name as we believe that the economics of the sector are based on exploration. For a brand to have value, it must generate lasting economic value, which is mainly the case in the consumer area. For an energy stock, removing advertising costs would not have a long-lasting effect on the business. This is also the case for telecoms, utilities, technology, financials and industrials. Conversely, R&D plays a fundamental role for industrials and technology, where the process is similar to pharmaceutical companies. Some of the R&D is capitalised when companies are using IAS, but the process is incomplete. For more on this matter, refer to the appendix of Chapter 8, Thematic investments – CROCI intellectual capital.

Adjustment four – estimate the correct life of the assets. The last important adjustment to valuation is estimating the economic life of the assets and applying the internal rate of return to predict the return on capital invested. Think of two companies, both requiring an investment of 100. One company produces a cash flow of 20 over 10 years and the other 20 over 20 years. The price of the two investments cannot be the same. One has an internal rate of return of 15% and the other one of 19%. It is thus essential to make a proper assessment of the assets' life.

Moving from a reported to an investment basis

Once such adjustments have been made, the investor will have a sound basis for making decisions. There are many challenges that the real investor still faces, but to help us on our journey through the remainder of the book, I will now use distinct terms to differentiate between Accounting concepts and Economic concepts (Fig. 2.7).

Accounting valuation	Investment-based valuation
Accounting P/E	**Economic P/E**
Not comparable across industries and sectors, or over time	Seeks true consistency and comparability between stocks, sectors and countries
$\text{Accounting } P/E = \dfrac{\text{Price/Book Value}}{\text{Return on Equity}}$	$\text{Economic } P/E = \dfrac{\text{EV/NCI}}{\text{CROCI}}$
Accounting inputs	Investment/economic inputs
Market capitalisation	**Enterprise Value**
Only includes the value of the equity, but ignores debt and other calls on shareholders	Includes not only financial debt but other liabilities, such as leases, warranties and pension underfunding
Book value	**Net capital invested**
Historical cost accounted. Ignores intangible economic assets, such as R&D and advertising of brands	Adjusted for inflation, and also includes capitalized intangibles, such as R&D and advertising of brands
Return on Equity	**Cash return on capital invested (CROCI)**
Does not represent an inflation-adjusted return. For example, depreciation is not charged economically, and asset life is inconsistent	The cash return over the life of the assets. Depreciation is charged economically, with similar assets having similar lives

FIGURE 2.7 Main adjustments required to move from accounting to economic valuation. *From DWS and CROCI.*

A peek at our due diligence process

To the reader who is familiar with the world of investment in equities and thinks of equities as pieces of companies, such a framework is intuitive. The process has been used by value investors for decades. However, it is a process that it is normally applied to a selective number of companies, perhaps up to 100. In our case, it is applied to nearly 1000 companies.

Applying such a process to regions and subsectors requires much in-depth knowledge of the economics of each sector and of different accounting standards and how they have evolved. Most importantly it is of fundamental importance that everyone concerned applies the process in a consistent manner; no personalisation being allowed. Research analysts need to think like a true investor who is performing the same due diligence on multiple companies eventually to take ownership of a few stocks out of the total universe of 1000.

This process has required time and training, and CROCI was lucky to be conceived by Miko Giedroyc, who was Head of Equity Research at Warburgs and later at Deutsche Morgan Grenfell, and by Pascal Costantini, the European and Global Strategist at Deutsche Morgan Grenfell and later DB Equities. They were able to ensure access to equity research analysts so we could understand and describe the economics of various sectors. In my early days, the primary task was capturing the knowledge that equity research analysts had. I started with the components of the DJIA, and as we grew we started a process of industrialising knowledge. Since 2009, this process has been run by Virginie Galas. She receives the support of our senior analysts based in Mumbai and led by Mital, Bharat, Yogendar, Venkat, Hussain, Mukarram, Gyan, Abhishek, Mahesh, Tathagat and Janamejay possess phenomenal knowledge about the economics of stocks and sectors. Vikash, Pragya and Pramod are masters in the systematic analysis of economic data and in the development of investment products. Michael and Anil make it possible through their IT expertise.

The analysis of Tokyo Electric Power (TEPCO) later in this chapter is illustrative of the fine work made on valuation. In other sectors, of course the knowledge differs. For pharmaceuticals, you need to have a good understanding of the research process associated with chemical or biological molecules. For Food and Beverage, brands and brand life are important. The final result must provide a consistent understanding of the real level of profitability, capital invested and valuation.

The job of the CROCI analyst is not to make calls, but to provide a sound economic analysis of companies and their valuations. If there are issues (with disclosure, for example) and the analysts cannot provide a sound framework for the economics of a company, they will suspend coverage. This happens rarely, but the principle is that you, as the potential owner, would not be comfortable in buying such a company. Suspension of work is more than justified.

Every year, coverage is reviewed as some companies become uninvestable, others are acquired, and still others emerge. It takes three people up to 1 month to start coverage of a single company. Their results are reviewed by the Head of Research. At any stage, we may decide to stop the process if what we see does not support our goal of owning part of a company. We can make adjustments to valuation, but we still need a sound basis. We know now that this due diligence process has on its own been a source of alpha. Companies are updated at least every other month, more often if necessary.

Since CROCI was invented by Deutsche Bank in 1996, many other companies have tried to imitate the process. Their approaches tend to be quantitative. Capitalisation of intangibles is over the same period for all. Leases are capitalised for 5–10 years, but in some cases this may lead to an underestimation of the assets. Accounting life is not adjusted. When asked what is different in what we do, my answer is that we do what a private equity investor or a potential acquirer normally does. It just happens to be applied to 1000 companies. What is certain is that CROCI is not a quant process.

The impact of such adjustments on valuation of sectors and regions

The effects of valuation adjustments can be significant and, as we can see in Fig. 2.8; these effects can also be revealing. Take Materials, Communication

Services and Energy, three sectors that have traditionally been classified as 'Value'. In the case of Gazprom, accounting based valuation ratios can quickly change once we make adjustments, as the median stocks in such sectors are actually at a premium to supposedly robust growth sectors such as Healthcare and IT! The valuation at the median level is much less attractive than it may appear, but the ranges are wild, going from companies that are in reality significantly cheaper than they appear to companies that can be $>3\times$ as expensive as they look.

	Median values		Impact on valuation (%)		
	CROCI PE	Accounting PE	Median	Min	Max
United States	28.8x	18.7x	48	−59	321
Europe	30.0x	18.3x	53	−80	344
Japan	25.2x	14.5x	60	−34	351
Rest of the world	30.2x	18.8x	50	−31	338
Comm. services	36.2x	15.6x	64	−16	317
Cons discretionary	27.1x	16.2x	49	−59	344
Cons staples	31.2x	21.7x	49	−23	279
Energy	28.7x	15.7x	81	−7	351
Healthcare	27.1x	19.1x	32	−34	218
Industrials	28.8x	18.0x	49	−80	319
IT	28.1x	19.0x	34	−38	338
Materials	29.2x	14.9x	62	−31	270
Utilities	29.4x	18.0x	65	−3	271

FIGURE 2.8   Adjusting accounts has a significant impact on valuation. *Data from DWS and CROCI.*

Some examples of adjustments and their impact on valuation

The last section of this chapter analyses in detail the adjustments made to four companies: Amazon, Celgene, Deutsche Lufthansa and Tokyo Electric Power (TEPCO). In each example, different issues must be addressed, but in each case the impact is relevant.

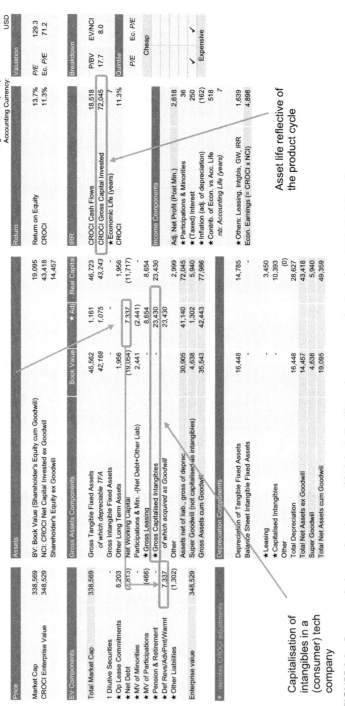

FIGURE 2.9 Some practical examples: Amazon (2016 data). For illustrative purposes only. *Data from DWS, CROCI and company accounts.*

Amazon

Amazon (Fig. 2.9) was a small company when it was first analysed and it appeared to be expensive, trading at a price-to-earnings ratio of close to 130 ×. The reality is more nuanced, however, as following our due diligence process the valuation of Amazon would actually fall to 71 × its level of 2016 earnings.

The difference in price was only 3%. Moving from Market Cap to an EV measure meant adding some financial liabilities associated to leasing commitments and removing some of the cash the company had, as it belonged to the sellers of the products on the Amazon platform.

The significant difference was in the level of capital invested in the business, which was north of 43bn USD (excluding goodwill), whilst the company recorded 14.4bn USD. Reinstating the leasing obligations on the balance sheet added 8.6bn, and including the financial liability for the products sold by third parties also meant that the net working capital was higher by another 7.3bn. The company was investing heavily in R&D, but those costs were expensed in the P&L. We estimated that it should be capitalised over 4 years, which added a further 12.5bn, with the remaining 1bn coming from adjustments to the tangible assets.

Amazon assets tend to have a short economic life, with tangible assets having an average of 7 years and the intangible assets having an average life of 4 years. Estimating the cash return on capital invested provided a cash return of 13.7% and a level of economic earnings of 4.9bn USD, higher than the official reported number of 2.6bn. This may come as a surprise, but the reader needs to consider that Amazon, a growth stock, was investing in its future. The level of R&D used to generate those revenues was significant below the level spent. The net result was a lower level of valuation than actually officially recorded, that is 71 × rather than 129 ×. Interestingly the adjusted price-to-book ratio (EV/NCI) was 8.0 × rather than 17.7 ×.

Celgene

Celgene (Fig. 2.10) is a biotech company, with significant spending on R&D, which according to the intrinsic logic of the sector would produce economic benefits in the distant future. As such, one would normally expect the company to capitalise the cost and then expense it, but because of the uncertainty associated with the process the accounting rule is to expense R&D in the P&L. This conservative approach reflects the principle of prudence in accounting and it made much sense in the 1950s, but over the past decades we have seen more and more information becoming available about the nature of the R&D process, about what companies are spending, and the life of drugs. In our approach, we use such information to define a tailored solution for each Healthcare company.

The price paid for the company goes up by 12% and the capital invested in the business goes from negative to positive (ex goodwill). Celgene in 2016 spent roughly USD 2.5bn in R&D, which we estimate has an economic life of 15 years. This means adding approximately USD 19.5bn of gross capital, which had been ramped up in previous years. This is one of the main sources for the significant increase in capital from a negative number of 9.3bn to a positive value of 15.7bn USD.

Originally it was not possible to calculate the value of the RoE, given the negative equity. We were able to estimate it at 29.8%, resulting in a real level of economic earnings of 4.7bn USD, higher than the reported number of 3.4bn USD. The difference can primarily be attributed to close to 1bn USD of expansionary capex and other adjustments.

The economic price-to-earnings ratio decreased from to $24.9\times$ to $20.4\times$. The impact on the price-to-book ratio was also relevant, as it went to $6.1\times$ operating capital, whilst before this was only represented by goodwill.

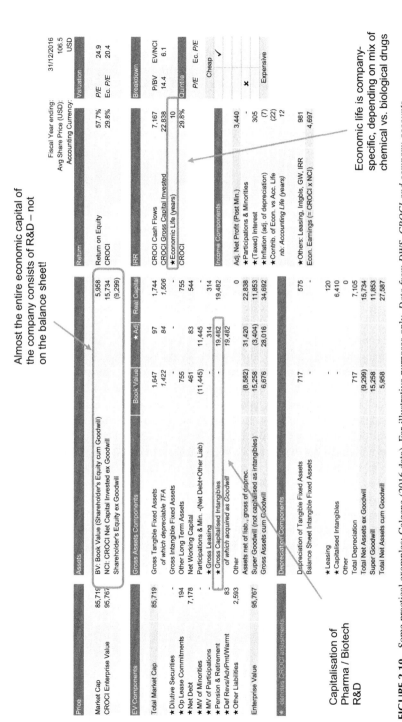

FIGURE 2.10 Some practical examples: Celgene (2016 data). For illustrative purposes only. *Data from DWS, CROCI and company accounts.*

Deutsche Lufthansa

Deutsche Lufthansa (Fig. 2.11) appeared very attractive on a *P/E* ratio of 4.8 × based on reported data in 2016. In reality, the company was on a CROCI-based *P/E* ratio of 32.4 × .

Our due diligence process revealed an elevated level of assets. Airlines commonly use a combination of owned and leased aircraft. Owned aircrafts are reported on balance sheets, but until recently aircraft that were on short-term leases were not reported. Both these categories of aircraft provide similar economic benefits to their operating airlines, but by not including one category of aircraft the reported financial statements can be misleading. In the case of Deutsche Lufthansa the gross tangible fixed assets (GTFA) was €34.9bn in 2016. This number increased by over €10bn by including various leased assets on the balance sheet. Inflation was another major adjustment, increasing the asset base by more than €4bn. At a practical level, it meant that the level of the net capital invested was €30.9bn.

CROCI's measure of capital includes debt and other financial liabilities, which are also capital but just funded differently. By means of CROCI's adjustments Deutsche Lufthansa's market value similarly increased fivefold from the value that is commonly used for assessing the price-to-earnings ratio. The market value of shares was €5.7bn but the EV that looks at the whole company and not just the equity shares was €25.7bn. The latter includes net debt of €3bn, which some market participants take into consideration, and also a debt that's built into operating lease commitments of €5.6bn and postretirement obligations of €6.3bn, amongst others.

The apparent undervaluation is from the underreporting of assets, including those on leases and the effects of inflation on the value of assets. The value for net assets excluding goodwill − a measure of the operating capital invested in the business − was reported at €3.7bn. After our adjustments these turned out to be 9 times larger, at €31bn. The company also had significant postretirement obligations that were commonly ignored. These are similar to financial debt and should be included in assessments of valuation as additional claimants on the profits generated by the business. By including such liabilities, the market value of Deutsche Lufthansa was nearly five times larger (EV €25.6bn) than just the market value of shares (Market Cap €5.7bn) which is commonly used in price-to-earnings calculations.

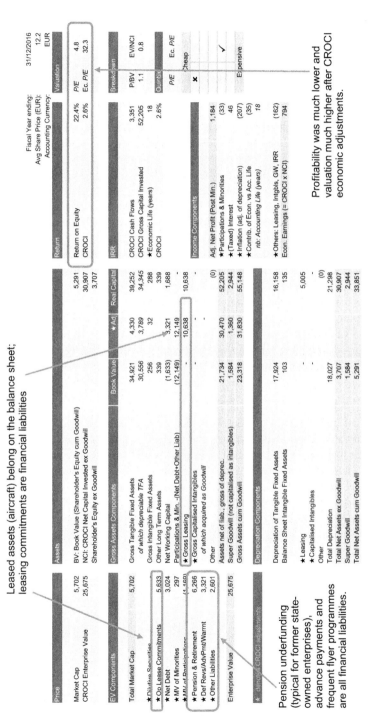

FIGURE 2.11 Some practical examples: Deutsche Lufthansa (2016 data). For illustrative purposes only. *Data from DWS, CROCI and company accounts*

Tokyo Electric Power (TEPCO) – a painful due diligence process

TEPCO (Fig. 2.15) generates, transmits and distributes electricity. The company uses hydroelectric, thermal and nuclear power sources. Because it is a utility, our focus was on the assets. Fig. 2.12 shows the breakdown that was available by looking at the balance sheet of the company in two different years, 1996 and 2011.

These notes do not provide any categorical breakdown of GTFA; Net Tangible Fixed Assets alone are disclosed by asset category. Accounts do not provide a categorical depreciation policy but only a brief overall depreciation policy. To our analyst, estimates for life and age made no sense. Given our intense focus on due diligence, there were other items that made no sense as well. Dividing the GTFA by the depreciation charge, one could have an estimate of the economic life for the company. In 1996 accounting life (calculated as GTFA divided by depreciation) was 21 years. That number was low compared to effective useful life of any power generation, transmission and distribution assets. In 2011 the same accounting life was 43 years. Wow, what a change! The company was using a depreciation method known as declining balance method, which skews the life and age calculation over the years and ultimately distorts both profitability and the value of the assets. Depreciation decreased from ¥1104 billion in 1996 to ¥699 billion in 2011, whereas gross depreciable tangible assets increased from ¥23,069 billion to ¥30,054 billion during the same period.

How CROCI approached the problem

To achieve an understanding of the economic value of a company, we ran a detailed analysis of each asset category and the power plants operated by the company, and we applied the effective useful life we observed in the industry. Our life assumptions were the result of years of research and documentation about various sectors, their typical asset constitution and their useful life. Using this information, we were able to estimate that between 1996 and 2012 the economic life went from 40 to 42 and the age climbed from 16 to 22, while reported data suggested that life grew from 21 to 43 and age increased from 11 to 32 (Fig. 2.13).

The impact on valuation (Fig. 2.14) was also notable. In the late 1990s the company was much more attractive on valuation ratios, and this was not the case at the end of 2009, when the stock was more expensive than it appeared.

	1996	2011
Gross property, plant and equipment	25,336	31,711
Less accumulated depreciation/amortization	12,321	22,130
Net property, plant and equipment	13,015	9,581

Property, plant and equipment (net), comprise of		
Hydroelectric power production facilities	575	646
Thermal power production facilities	1,363	850
Nuclear power production facilities	1,513	726
Transmission facilities	T3,030	2,010
Transformation facilities	1,217	787
Distribution facilities	2,310	2,125
General facilities	269	143
Other electricity-related PP&E	40	89
Other property, plant and equipment	221	417
Construction in progress	1,925	944
Nuclear fuel	550	845
Net property, plant and equipment	13,015	9,581

Results	1996	2011
Accounting life*	21	43
Account age**	11	32
Economic life	40	42
Economic age	16	22

FIGURE 2.12   TEPCO: composition of GTFA for the year ended. *Data from DWS, CROCI and company accounts. Notes: *Calculated as (depreciable PP&E/annual depreciation charge) and **Calculated as (accumulated depreciation/annual depreciation charge).*

	Capacity (MW)	Operation began	Years in operation	Years remaining	% of total capacity
Hydro power plants (economic life—80years)					
Imaichi	1,050	1988	29	51	2
Shiobara	900	1994	23	57	1
Tanbara	1,200	1970	47	33	2
Plant details removed for clarity					
Azumi	623	1990	28	53	1
Shin-Takasegawa	1,280	1955	62	18	2
Kazunogawa	1,200	2000	18	63	2
Total hydro power plants	**9,872**		**35**	**45**	**16**
Nuclear power plants (economic life—40years)					
Fukushimia Daini	4,400	1982	36	5	7
Kashiwazaki-Kariwa	8,212	1991	26	14	13
Total nuclear power plants	**12,612**		**29**	**11**	**20**
Thermal power plants (economic life—40years)					
Chiba	4,380	2000	17	23	6
Anegasaki	3,600	1973	40	0	6
Sodegaura	3,600	1976	40	0	6
Futtsu	5,040	1992	25	15	8
Plant details removed for clarity					
Kashima	5,660	1994	21	19	9
Hirono	4,400	1992	26	15	7
Kawasaki	3,420	2008	9	31	5
Total thermal power plants	**41,155**		**24**	**16**	**65**
Total power plants	**63,690**	Econ. age 27years		Econ. life 43years	
Total tan. assets (incl transmis. and distrib.)		Econ. age 23years		Econ. life 40years	

FIGURE 2.13   TEPCO: plant details. *Data from DWS, CROCI and company accounts.*

Before	1996	1997	1998		2009	2010	2011	2012
Price/book value	2.35	1.99	2.27		1.32	2.03	0.63	0.80
Return on equity	5.3%	8.7%	6.4%		5.2%	12.0%	-33.4%	-13.8%
Accounting *P/E*	44.5	23.0	35.5		25.3	16.9	NM	NM
After								
EV/NCI	0.66	0.67	0.67		0.68	0.72	0.57	0.61
CROCI	2.9%	3.4%	2.9%		1.9%	1.9%	-0.8%	-0.6%
Economic PE	22.9	20.0	22.8		36.9	38.8	NM	NM

FIGURE 2.14   TEPCO: impact of CROCI on valuation. *Data from DWS, CROCI and company accounts.*

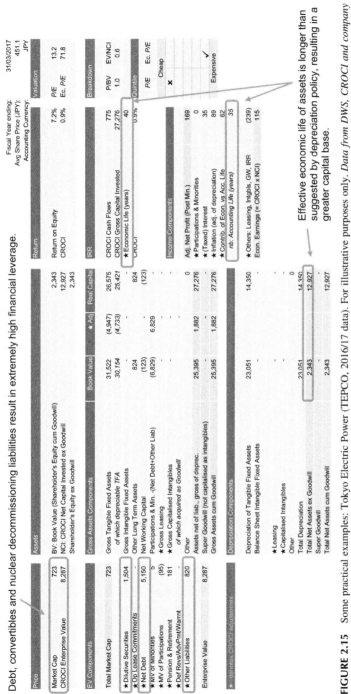

FIGURE 2.15 Some practical examples: Tokyo Electric Power (TEPCO, 2016/17 data). For illustrative purposes only. *Data from DWS, CROCI and company accounts.*

Chapter 3

The analytical idiosyncrasies of banks

Chapter Outline

The 23 May 2018 was an important date for our team. After 22 years, we finally launched our valuation framework for banks. It will still take a few more years before we do the same for insurance companies but maybe not in my working lifetime. This may sound absurd in the world of real-time information and the Internet, but our approach has always concentrated on performing due diligence and deciding on the valuation of listed stocks. This approach applies to industrials, banks and insurance. If we are not comfortable with the underlying material, we do not proceed. No shortcuts are taken, and there is simply not enough information for us to compare insurance companies to the rest of the market. In this chapter, I talk about how we analyse banks and why the process took so long. This chapter draws heavily on a report[1] published on 23 May 2018, which launched coverage on banks. The content and framework have not changed.

Banks, an important sector filled with valuation ambiguities

Banks are critical to the functioning of an economy. They connect owners of financial capital to those in need of it and facilitate transactions. New

---

1. CROCI Focus: Banks, DWS, May 2018. All rights reserved. Any unauthorised use is prohibited.

Valuing and Investing in Equities. DOI: https://doi.org/10.1016/B978-0-12-813848-9.00003-0
39

technologies are reshaping banking, but even though it is now possible to imagine a world where technology itself is able to connect providers of capital directly with the users, we still cannot imagine a modern economy without a properly functioning financial system. The central importance of the banking sector is reflected in its representation in major equity benchmarks. The financial sector makes up 20.7% of FTSE Developed index capitalisation with banks alone accounting for nearly half (9.2%) of this.[2] In the past, the banking sector accounted for an even larger proportion of the market capitalisation within these benchmarks.

Broadly speaking, the importance of the banking sector is well understood by investors. But its financials present a somewhat murkier picture. The challenges are such that even well-regarded investors have had their fingers burnt by the sector. Readers may recall Warren Buffett's lucrative provision of capital to distressed banks after the financial crisis (Goldman Sachs, Bank of America). Perhaps fewer readers will recall that in 2008 he lost money in banks. In Berkshire Hathaway's 2008 Annual report he wrote: *During 2008, I spent $244m for shares of two Irish banks that appeared cheap to me. At year end we wrote these holdings down to market: $27m, for an 89% loss. Since then, the two stocks have declined even further. The tennis crowd would call my mistakes 'unforced errors'.*[3]

We certainly have still much to learn from the Sage of Omaha. However, his 2008 loss still highlights the challenges that investors face. Take valuations, for example – banks always appear to be better value than the rest of the market. For value investors, the question is *why* such an anomaly would persist in an efficient market, and over several decades? In a 'normal' market value opportunities do not persist over the long term since capital chases the extra return and that removes the valuation asymmetries.

Investors face additional challenges when analysing banks' financial statements. These primarily arise from the nature of banks' operations, which differ substantially from those of nonfinancial companies. There are three distinct components:

1. Cash is a financial asset for nonfinancial companies. For banks, however, cash is an operating asset, much like merchandise for a retailer. When cash can also be an operating asset this approach breaks down as it is difficult to separate operating cash from financial cash. As a result, investors face serious difficulties in analysing the cash returns banks are generating for their shareholders.
2. The valuation of a bank's assets also presents problems. There are challenges in determining the book or carrying value of loans and other

---

2. Data from Bloomberg Finance L.P. The 20.7% weight of Financials includes Real Estate which made up 2.8% of the index Data as available on 23 May 2018.
3. Berkshire Hathaway, 2008 AR, page 16.

operating assets. Banks are required to estimate likely losses on their loan books and create provisions by charging these losses as expenses. However, discretion is required to estimate such losses, something which has traditionally created opportunities for banks to manage their reported profits. External investors generally struggle to obtain the necessary information to analyse these provisions objectively and completely.

3. Banks are riskier than the market perceives. A common fallacy is that banks are less risky investments than comparable nonfinancial companies. The notion that they have lower risk might come from their lower bond yields or even from their CDS spreads, which are substantially below those of their nonfinancial counterparts. However, the profitability of a bank is, in a simplified framework, a function of the amount of times the equity component is levered and the interest margin [crudely, Return on Equity (ROE) = leverage $\times$ interest margin, i.e., 3% spread between loans and deposits $\times$ 10 $\times$ equity = 30%]. If you increase the leverage, the ROE will increase, and banks have historically been highly levered. To put this into context, in 2018 the Bank of England required most UK banks to have at least 3% of their assets funded by equity capital. This means a possible 33 $\times$ financial leverage and also that a mere 3% loss of their loan book can wipe out all of their equity.

This high leverage exists because banks play a fundamental role in connecting savers with borrowers. High leverage may be desirable economically, as it means that a low interest margin can be sustained between loans and deposits, but it also brings risks. An economic downturn can potentially wipe out its entire equity base. The alternative − low leverage − is not desirable as banks would be forced to increase interest margins so they can remunerate providers of capital at risk, which could potentially choke off the economy as the benchmark for investments would rise. In this role, there is a balancing act between intermediation margin, risk and return. Whilst it is true that banks may have more backstops than nonfinancial companies, individual banks can fail just as easily if they misjudge their loss exposure.

CROCI and banks

CROCI was set up with the initial focus of defining a valuation framework that enabled comparisons across sectors and markets. Work first started in the early 1990s, but the official launch date was 1996. The notable exception was financials, and this situation remained until 2018. Since 1996, investors have regularly asked why financials were excluded. The answer was simple: the time was not ripe.

CROCI is a fundamental approach and creating a framework for financials required information that is not available for the type of work conducted by a real investor. Our objective has never been to cover every possible corner of the market but rather to focus on segments that we can value objectively. Historically, financials have been poor at disclosing information, especially where their balance sheets were concerned. As a result it made sense for us to focus on other parts of the market rather than build a good model on opaque financial statements.

The situation differs by components in the financial sector. In the banking sector the Basel frameworks have improved disclosure and risk management standards.

The creation of a CROCI banks model

Our analyses regularly assessed the possibility of launching coverage. In 2005 a CROCI Banks task force was established. After close scrutiny, it recommended that the best decision was to wait until a regulatory framework permitted better disclosure for analysing capital. It was nevertheless clear that a different type of model would be required. A bank can be thought of as two businesses, one managing liabilities (deposits and loans) where the payments are certain and another managing assets (loans and financial investments) with varying risk profiles. Investors in a bank do not own the net assets in a bank; instead they own the equity − the riskiest component. This is the part that could easily be wiped out should things turn sour. Equity is a function of the total assets employed in a business and associated risk ratios that are used to estimate risk-weighted assets (RWAs). The concept of RWAs, in theory, neutralises the differences in risk profile between different institutions and (again in theory) enables comparability across banks, but in the past this has been a target rather than reality.

So why did we deem inadequate attempts to neutralise risk? In 1988 the Basel Accord was published. This standard required banks to hold at least 8% of their RWAs in Tier 1 capital (equity). However, risks were defined too broadly. Assets were classified into broad categories and the same risk weighting was applied to them even though individual assets within those categories varied significantly in terms of credit quality. Hence full comparability was not possible. Basel II (2004) allowed more detailed calibration of risk. Basel II was a major improvement over the preceding standard. Risk categories were refined and capital was more closely tied to the risk that banks actually undertook. However, it allowed banks to use their own risk models, which created incentives to underestimate risk. At a practical level, the framework gave too much discretion to individual banks and underestimated the conflict of interest existing for management. This approach proved catastrophic during the 2008 crisis, as demonstrated by the large-scale recapitalisation of banks after the financial crisis.

The postcrisis financial reforms — Basel III

The financial crisis was a watershed moment for banks and led to a raft of regulations aiming to strengthen their capital requirements and increasing banks transparency. The changes included:

1. Calculation of RWAs: Basel III places significant constraints on the use of internal models by banks. In several risk categories, only standardised models can be used.[4] This corrects a major shortcoming of the Basel II standard, which allowed banks to use internal-risk ratings to calculate their RWAs. As capital levels are defined in relation to the RWAs that banks hold, the internal ratings-based approach allows banks significant leeway in determining their own RWAs, and hence their capital levels. This makes it practically impossible for outsiders to determine and compare capital levels across the banks.

2. Capital requirements used to be evaluated based on three tiers (1−3). Basel III eliminates Tier 3 and split Tier 1 capital into two types − Common Equity Tier 1 (CET1) consisting of equity and Additional Tier 1 consisting of contingent convertibles.

   Under Basel III, capital definitions have become stricter. CET1 basically consists of shareholders equity, but is subject to several newly included deductions (such as certain types of deferred tax assets and the majority of intangible assets).

3. Introduction of additional buffers: In addition to the higher capital requirement, Basel III introduced additional capital buffers such as the mandatory capital conservation buffer, the countercyclical buffer and the globally systematically important bank (GSIB) buffer. All three buffers serve different purposes but the capital conservation buffer, by virtue of being mandatory, has already had a substantial impact on banks.

Thanks to these changes, comparability across the sector has improved dramatically. We estimate that common equity may have been raised by over 50% from prefinancial crisis levels (Fig. 3.1).

In addition, Basel III introduces fully new concepts outside the ambit of pure capital requirements:

- Leverage ratio − 3% outside United States and 5% in the United States − measured against total assets (rather than RWAs).
- Two liquidity ratios, the Liquidity Coverage Ratio and the Net Stable Funding Ratio, forcing banks to maintain large pools of liquid assets.

---

4. Recent Basel III amendments to be implemented starting 2022 also place a floor on the RWA calculated using the banks' internal models. The floor is set at 72.5% of the RWA given by standardised models.

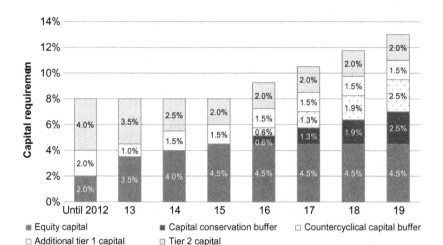

FIGURE 3.1 Bank capital requirement under Basel rules. *Data from DWS, Basel Committee on Banking Supervision.*

After Basel III

Improving the quantity and quality of banks' capital was everyone's immediate focus after the financial crisis. Basel III shifted the focus towards monitoring banks' financial health and improving their resilience for future adverse economic and financial conditions. Regulators in the United States and Europe now periodically stress test banks capital levels to assess whether banks hold sufficient capital to survive such situations.

This monitoring framework, however, is arduous for banks and regulators alike. Efforts have begun to simplify the process. For example, the Federal Reserve has recently published proposals to streamline banks' capital by combining the requirements under its Comprehensive Capital Analysis and Review (CCAR) with the buffer requirements in the Capital Rule. The Federal Reserve also proposed a new stress leverage buffer to replace the current requirement under the CCAR process where banks need to demonstrate their ability to maintain capital levels above minimum requirements under stress situations.

These proposals would align banks' capital requirements more closely with firm specific risks. At the level of smaller banks, these new proposals would reduce the capital requirements but for the GSIBs, the new proposals would mean an additional USD 10bn to 50bn in aggregate capital.

The results of a more tightly defined framework for capital requirements have provided a higher degree of confidence about the quality of company disclosure. This confidence has always been a crucial element in determining the inclusion of companies in the CROCI database. The move to Basel III's calculation of RWAs in particular was an essential step on this journey.

Difficulties in covering the insurance subsector

Financial reporting still remains poor in parts of the Financials sector. To help remedy that, the International Accounting Standards Board (IASB) recently published IFRS 17 for the insurance sector. The new standard will become effective from January 2021 and is a major step toward making insurance companies' accounts comparable on a global basis.

In the insurance sector, there have been even greater difficulties in comparing companies thanks to a multitude of opaque national reporting practices. These inconsistencies have prevented CROCI from issuing an authoritative analysis of the sector. But now, after two decades of negotiation, the IASB has announced a substantial accounting change to harmonise the treatment of insurance companies.

The introduction of a uniform international accounting standard means that insurers in over 100 countries will face a substantial accounting change at the outset of 2021 that should make the sector less impregnable and more investible − and may well even lower the cost of capital. This new rule will affect 450 listed insurers who manage $13 trillion in assets. Whilst this will not affect the United States, similar work is also being carried out there.

CROCI's adjustments to the valuation of banks

The standard CROCI model is of limited use for banks. Investors in bank shares are primarily owners of banks' equity capital rather than their assets, as they are for nonfinancial companies. Banks have no real distinction between their financial and operating assets, as well as high levels of leverage. For banks, equity capital is typically the minimum amount necessary to underpin a loan business at a specified risk level. Even so, the basic principles behind CROCI still hold. In many ways these principles are easier to apply to banks than to nonfinancial companies. Due diligence is still required to establish the economic capital and the profitability of that capital, but the process is less onerous.

Adjustment one − the capital base. Significant advances have been made in strengthening banks' capital requirements and building credibility around that capital since the financial crisis. A raft of regulations aimed at reducing systemic risks and greater oversight from regulators has meant that capital is now better and more uniformly defined across markets − a good starting point for CROCI-type analysis. However, certain adjustments are still necessary to remove capital inconsistencies. These are most relevant for cross-border comparisons but are also necessary when comparing banks of different sizes.

Deferred Tax Assets (DTAs) are an example of one such adjustment. These assets (and liabilities) arise from temporary differences in accounting for various income and expenses between financial statements prepared under accounting rules and those for tax returns. Operating losses in one period which can be offset against taxable income in future periods are a major source of these assets. Basel III requires banks to deduct all DTAs arising from the carryover of past operating losses from their Core Equity Tier 1 (CET1) capital. Any remaining DTAs in excess of 10% of CET1 capital must also be excluded. Some national regulators have tweaked their rules to reclassify DTA as another asset to enable their supervisee banks to circumvent this requirement and improve their capital ratios. To compare capital levels uniformly, we remove this favourable treatment and deduct DTAs in excess of 10% CET1 capital from reported capital in all our coverage of banks.

The recent US tax code change further reduces the amount of DTAs on banks' books. For most banks, this change reduces their regulatory capital but its impact varies from bank to bank depending on the level of their DTAs.

Adjustment two − net profits. Cash flows are measured after tax, consistent with the capital invested calculation. We add back cash flow (after tax) relating to Tier One debt, minority interest and the like. The interest cost and expected return from plan assets for pensions and postretirement benefits are normalised based on the funded status of the company. This adjustment removes the management's expectation of expected return from plan assets and considers a realistic return in our analysis. Private equity gains and losses in excess of acceptable trend limits are also reversed. Litigation charges are treated as normal business expenditure, even if the amount is very significant. The strict regulatory framework of the business demands the entire sector be discounted for litigation costs.

Adjustment three − inflation. The adjustments to capital and cash flows that we have discussed so far remove most of the inconsistencies that exist in the reported financial statements of banks. But the adjustment for inflation is still missing. On the surface, inflation may not seem as problematic for banks as, unlike nonfinancial companies, assets are primarily monetary which are reported at their actual values in the books.

This distinguishing characteristic of banks certainly saves us a lot of trouble in estimating the actual value of their capital. However, it does not mean that inflation does not distort banks' profitability as it does at nonfinancial companies. Banks' capital is invested in nominal and not real terms. So the returns banks generate are also nominal whose value would vary depending on the rate of inflation.

To illustrate this point, consider two banks, A and B. The former operates in a country where inflation is 2% whilst the latter operates in a country where inflation is 10%. Because of the higher inflation, Bank B would have to earn 8% more than Bank A in any given year to be at par with Bank A. This would be the case as assets of both these banks are mainly monetary whose value would depreciate with inflation. These assets would be recorded at their current market value in the banks' books but their purchasing power would be lower because of inflation. To compare banks in different geographies and across time, their profitability needs to be adjusted for this loss of purchasing power.

Therefore using the excess of money supply growth over GDP growth or the GDP deflator, we charge the cash flows for the loss of value of banks' monetary assets from inflation.

Adjustment four — enterprise value. Our definition of market value is very close to market capitalisation. However, to be consistent with earnings, the market capitalisation is adjusted for unrecognised gains from industrial holdings, private equity and other strategic investments. We also consider Tier 1 debt and fair value of minorities as part of enterprise value.

Adjustment five — the discount rate. The adjustments described so far result in consistent information for three of the four components that are necessary to appraise banks' valuations. That just leaves the discount rate. I will go through the details of the discount rate for nonfinancial companies in Chapter 4, Stock picking based on economic fundamentals, what is relevant at this stage is to highlight that the discount rate differs for bank. This means that when comparing valuation with nonfinancial sectors, we must adjust for differences in the discount rate. The difference in the discount rate is a function of the risk embedded when buying a bank's equity. The best way to think about the discount rate versus industrials is to think of credit and to compare the valuation of an AAA with a BB. It is normal to expect a gap in valuation, but it will not make the BB cheap versus AAA, it is just an indication of a difference in risk profile. The same applies to banks versus nonfinancial companies. While investors ought to expect a return of 5.4% on nonfinancials, an additional adjustment is necessary to reward the investors for the higher risks associated to the substantially higher level of leverage for banks. Equity capital for nonfinancial companies is typically levered between one and three times. However, at banks, this same capital can be levered up to 22 ×, which requires an additional premium. *To estimate the extra premium, we look at the long-term ROE for banks as the long-term ROE will necessarily converge to what the providers of financial capital will demand.* The US Federal Deposit Insurance Corporation has aggregate net income and equity capital levels for US banks going back to 1934. Using these along with the World Bank's inflation data, we are able to calculate an inflation-adjusted ROE for US banks over the entire period since 1934 (Fig 3.2). By analysing the ROE of banks and using the equivalence principle that in an efficient market the long-term return must equal the cost of capital (as well as investors' required return on investment), we calculate that the cost of capital has averaged around 7.5% over the long term after adjusting for inflation. The ROE of US banks has averaged 6.4% since 1934. However, the returns in the early part of this series were affected by the turbulence generated by the Great Depression and then the Second World War. Excluding this period and adjusting for the lower risk profile of banks currently suggests a long-term expected return of 7.5%.

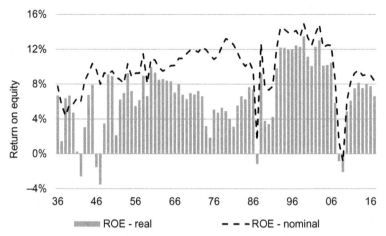

FIGURE 3.2 Inflation-adjusted ROE and nominal ROE of the US commercial banks. *Data from Federal Deposit Insurance Corporation, DWS and CROCI.*

Readers should also note the wide gap between the reported and real ROEs of the US banks in 1970s. High levels of inflation reduced their actual profitability, since equity in a bank is a nominal asset.

The impact of our adjustments on valuation and terms of comparison with nonfinancial companies

CROCI adjusts the price-to-earnings ratios of banks by a ratio of long-term cost of capital of Financials (7.5%) to that of nonfinancial companies (5.4%). Whatever is the valuation of a bank, post our adjustment, it needs to be multiplied by a factor of 138.9% to make it comparable to a nonfinancial company. This adjustment expressly accounts for the higher risk premium of banks and puts their valuations on a level playing field with the rest of CROCI's coverage. This removes the inherent bias towards financial stocks in systematic strategies and allows CROCI strategies to select stocks on their individual merits.

The adjustments made to the Book, the ROE and the price are important as they increase the *P/E* by almost 20%, but the real difference is made by the adjustment to the discount factor, increasing the valuation by close to 39%. These adjustments are not made in the world of index or passive investing, where analysts routinely tend to overstate the values of financial stocks (Fig. 3.3).

For example, at the end of 2017 the S&P 500 Index had a 15% weight in the financial sector. At that same time, the S&P 500 Value index, which provides exposure to the value stocks within the broader index, had almost twice that weight (25%) in the sector. Whilst we understand the overweighting of the Financials sector, it's worth noting that S&P's assessment of value was

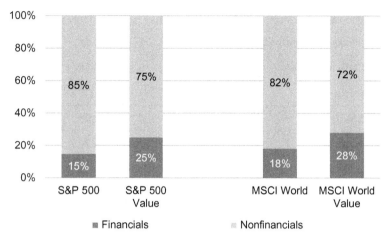

FIGURE 3.3 Weight of financials in commonly used value benchmarks. *Data from Factset Research Systems, Bloomberg Finance L.P.*

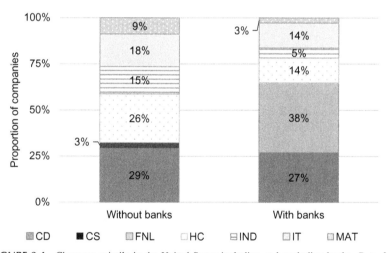

FIGURE 3.4 Cheapest quintile in the United States including and excluding banks. *Data from DWS and CROCI. The stock ranking is determined by their 2018 Economic P/E (Adjusted P/E in the case of Banks).*

based on three factors, one of which was earnings-to-price ratio. As this ratio was not adjusted for the higher risk premium of Financials sector, we argue it overstated the Value Score of the sector. A similar discrepancy exists in the MSCI World Value index, which uses a similar Value Score based on unadjusted earnings-to-price ratios.

We are now ready to look at the relative valuation of stocks (Fig 3.4) and the sector. In aggregate, banks currently trade on a *P/E* of 13.5 ×; adjusted for its higher cost of capital, the *P/E* increases to 18.7 ×. The latter is

Economic P/E and adj. P/E	2018	2013–18 avg.
Consumer discretionary	29.3×	26.5×
Consumer staples	26.2×	28.3×
Banks	13.5× (18.7×)	13.8× (19.2×)
Energy	31.5×	46.9×
Health care	20.6×	22.2×
Industrials	25.0×	25.8×
Information technology	24.4×	20.9×
Materials	23.6×	27.2×
Telecommunication services	26.5×	31.6×
Utilities	29.1×	26.9×

FIGURE 3.5 Global sectors *P/E*: economic *P/E* 2018 and 5-year avg. *Data from DWS and CROCI; company accounts. The figures in parenthesis are adjusted for Bank's higher cost of capital.*

comparable to the Economic *P/E* of nonfinancial companies, which trade at 24.6 ×. This puts banks at a discount of over a third to the broader market. To put the valuation of banks further into context, the next cheapest sector globally is Health Care which is on an Economic *P/E* of 20.6 × (Fig. 3.5).

Epilogue: banks and the financial crisis

The 2008−09 crisis fundamentally changed the way banks operate. In many respects, though, such an event is nothing new. I do not even have to look as far back as the Great Depression for the last precedent (US savings and loan crisis 1986−95, Finnish banking crisis 1990s, Swedish banking crisis 1990s, Latam financial crises 1990s and Asian financial crisis 1997). In 2007, years of low inflation, stable growth and accommodative monetary policies created a perfect storm, resulting in a surge in debt levels thereby paving the way for an eventual crash. Hyman Minsky described this behaviour in his financial instability hypothesis. He talked of three forms of financing. First, the safest form of financing − 'hedge financing' − in which companies rely on their future cash flows to repay all their borrowings. The other two are riskier, namely, 'speculative financing' and 'Ponzi financing'. In the former, companies rely on their cash flows to repay interest but must roll over their debt to repay the principal. In 'Ponzi financing' companies rely on additional debt to repay both the interest and the principal on additional debt (see Chapter 10: Bubbles in equities).

As the business cycle matures, risk appetite increases. Both corporates and investors take on additional debt to feed their growing risk appetite. This behaviour works for a while, as with additional leverage the profitability of their capital increases. At the macro level, however, this behaviour pushes the economy further and further away from its trend path, causing stresses to build up and almost always ending in a crash. Financial markets tend to have short memories, though — this hypothesis was published in 1992 and the financial crisis happened in 2008. In between, there was also the bursting of the TMT bubble. So the 2008–09 financial crisis was not the first crisis to hurt banks profitability and won't be the last.

The high water mark for banks' return on capital was 2007. For the whole of the previous decade, returns had been very high by historical standards, hovering around the 20% level. This high profitability was aided by:

- rising leverage,
- multidecade lows in provisions for loan losses,
- peak levels in the loan-to-deposit ratio (a measure of liquidity risk),
- peak levels in the contribution to profitability from noninterest income.

But, alongside these high levels of profitability, warning signals foretold that the elevated trend was not sustainable. US bank leverage swelled to 15.6×. The ability of banks to set their own capital requirements was exploited under the constant pressure to improve returns. Banks were able to classify certain debt instruments as equity even if they did not have the same loss-absorbing capacity as equity. Balance sheets were able to expand dramatically without any strong regulatory constraints.[5] As a result of lax capital requirements, total US indebtedness rose from 13.8× tangible equity to 15.6×. Banks believed they could grow without taking on extra risk, according to some commentators. In reality, the culture of risk-taking by global banks dramatically increased. Combined with a long period of low inflation and economic growth, this culture encouraged consumers' belief that increasing debt levels had very little risk attached. While risks were on the rise, there were no liquidity requirements under the prevailing regulatory framework (Basel II), which left individual banks to determine how much of their assets should be liquid. The combination of various factors (higher risk, poor liquidity and vulnerable framework) led to the financial crisis.

The introduction of Basel III's increased capital and liquidity requirements has substantially reduced financial leverage in the sector. The Tier 1 ratio has risen from 8% in 2006 to 14% in 2018. This rise has had clear

---

5. Although banks must shoulder some blame for the financial crisis, they were certainly not alone in causing it. Central banks and regulators also played a role, through a very loose regulatory framework.

negative implications for profitability, but lower net interest margins (a consequence of the extra liquidity injected into the market by central banks) also had an effect. Together these two phenomena have pushed returns on capital down to around half their level before the financial crisis — around 10% in 2018 compared to 20% in 2006.

Chapter 4

Stock picking based on economic fundamentals

Chapter Outline

A systematic due diligence of companies' accounts provides an excellent basis for the investment process. However, the value of a company ought to be the discounted net present value of earnings [or discounted cash flows models (DCFs)] that the company will produce over its life. The focus, therefore, ought to be on future earnings.

In attempting to evaluate the future prospects of the business, most investors create a valuation model that combines their own analysis with the services provided by equity research analysts.

$$P = E(y_1) + E(y_2) + \cdots + E(y_n) \quad \text{discounted to today's value}$$

Equity research includes a vast pool of professional researchers who provide industry analysis, company insights and recommendations based on forward-looking valuation models. The reports associated with valuation models are impressive both in their level of analysis and complexity. This depth of reporting facilitates forecasts of future earnings and their dynamics. However, there is considerable controversy about the value of such process. This position is best argued by Eugene Fama: *Ultimately, in a DCF calculation, you've got cash flows in the numerator, which are random variables, and you've got another random variable in the denominator. At this point, a*

Valuing and Investing in Equities. DOI: https://doi.org/10.1016/B978-0-12-813848-9.00004-2
53

statistician's hair is standing on the end because you've got a ratio of two random variables. In the end, we have no evidence that the whole process is any better than a rule of thumb (*Journal of Applied Corporate Finance*, Volume 28, Number 4, Fall 2016, p. 13).

Fama is a staunch proponent of the efficient market theory (EMT), in which there is no role for fundamental analysis. The underlying argument of proponents of the EMT is that the value of extracting alpha through a fundamental process is offset by the costs of the process associated with it − in a nutshell it is a futile exercise. It is an argument partially supported by the lack of performance on average from active management. Still, there are several flaws in the EMT. Fama's own work is based on accounting data, whose flaws I have demonstrated and there is a simple solution to the *randomness* associated to the cost of capital. Instead of trying to estimate the costs of capital with company, sector and market beta, one could be simply measure the expected rate of return demanded by those providing capital at risk. In the end, if markets are efficient, capital will flow and any excess return will be competed away to the point that return and risks across sectors and markets will be normalised.

The challenges of looking at the future

In any case, Fama has a point when it comes to challenges of estimating future earnings. Given a discount rate, estimating the value of a stock requires precise information about future earnings and the life of the company. Our analysis suggests that, even assuming that one knows the exact discount rate, an accurate estimate of the life of the company and its cash flows is close to impossible.

Take, for instance, the components of the Dow Jones Industrial Average in 1959 (I will analyse this matter in Chapter 8: Thematic investments − CROCI intellectual capital). This is an exclusive circle dedicated to the best of the best. Still, out of the 30 stocks listed in 1959, Sears, General Motors, Texaco, Bethlehem Steel, Chrysler and Eastman Kodak have filed for bankruptcy. I do not have any models from those times, but I doubt any research analyst was able to forecast when and why their bankruptcies took place. If you were to look at the components of the DJIA today, I doubt you would find any model that assumes that 20% of current components will be bankrupt in 50 years!

The complexity increases as earnings associated with the distant future have a significant impact on valuation. Fig. 4.1 shows the example of a few companies producing 100 of constant earnings over their lives, with a discount rate of 5%. Each company has a different life (10, 25, 50 and 100 years). For a company with 25 years of life, 45% of the value is from years 11 to 25. Still research analysts mostly provide forecasts for the next 2 years, but earnings for the next 2 years represent 13% of the value of a company with a life of 25 years!

Economic Life	Perpetuity	100 years	50 years	25 years	10 years
Earnings	100	100	100	100	100
Discount rate	5%	5%	5%	5%	5%
Fair value	2000	1985	1826	1409	772.2
Fair value P/E ratio	20x	19.8x	18.3x	14.1x	7.8x
Value in the next 10 years	38%	39%	42%	55%	100%
Value between year 11 and 25	32%	32%	35%	45%	
Value between year 26 and 50	21%	21%	23%		
Value between year 51 and 100	8%	8%			
Value beyond 100 years	1%				

FIGURE 4.1 How life expectancy affects valuation ratios and how much of the valuation is about earnings in the long term. *From the author.*

One could argue that equity research analysts with their expertise are able to forecast the future through their recommendations, but this is not the case. The lowest number of buy recommendations for the S&P500 was in April 2009, with the S&P 500 at 873. It has since more than tripled! If you were to look at the history of recommendations for Nokia, Microsoft and Blackberry, the highest numbers of buy recommendations coincided with the highest prices, and the lowest numbers of buy recommendations with the lowest prices, which has to be understood as the industry's massive failure to provide insights about the future (Fig. 4.2). The case of Microsoft is particularly intriguing. The stock tripled in the past 5 years, the number of buys went from 14 to 34 and the stock went from cheap to expensive as the Economic *P/E* ratio went from 19.7 $\times$ to 32.4 $\times$.

		At the highest level of price			At the lowest level of price		
	Ccy	Price	Date	# Buy/ Sell	Price	Date	# Buy/ Sell
Nokia	EUR	28.6	07-Nov-07	59%/16%	1.371	18-Jul-12	22%/37%
Blackberry	USD	147.55	19-Jun-08	75%/3%	5.75	09-Dec-13	5%/37%
Microsoft	USD	130.6	30-Apr-19	89%/5%	15.15	09-Mar-09	68%/0%

FIGURE 4.2 Buys and sells recommendations at high and low points. *Data from Bloomberg Finance L.P.*

The focus on short-term dynamics is further amplified by sales and trading groups. I occasionally receive emails from sales and trading businesses. The noise you get from the industry is deafening! Here is an edited example:

XYZ is reporting tomorrow!!!! Focus sheet

XYZ is reporting tomorrow and this is our focus sheet. Our analyst remains bullish and the number will be sound, but the stock may have already performed very strongly and even if the technicals are good, sentiment is turning down. The stock may rally after the numbers but this may be short lived.

Technicals
Medium term analysis: Shares have closed up in 10 out of the last 13 earnings releases
Short-term analysis: Shares have closed up in 3 out of the last 3 earnings releases
Options market: Implying a 3% move versus average move of 2.4% over the past six quarters

Performance
Stock is up 40% since the October lows; 15% year-to-date; peer group is up 20% and 10% and sector +17% and 8%.

Analyst
The analysts is still bullish on the stock and has done some channels check suggesting that demand for the products is still strong, with the company expecting to beat consensus

Sentiment survey
The stock is now out of the 10 long in our market survey, having consistently been in the top 10 for the last four quarters

Stock analysis based on price, earnings and the discount rate

I agree with Fama. DCF based valuation frameworks are something to wish for, something that can help the decision making process, but it is best to recognise their limits. If I could, I would get rid of recommendations, DCFs and share price targets.

Tenet #8 of our investment framework: it is better to have no valuation model than a beautiful model with precisely wrong earnings forecasts.

But giving up forecasts does not mean giving up fundamental analysis. The kind of fundamental analysis that I propose provides investors with the tools for investment decisions and lets the investor decide. Here is what I suggest as being the fundamental steps in such process:

- Understand the discount rate (the dark side of valuation) and how it affects the price of equities.

- Have clarity about how price, earnings and discount rates interact as well as their impact on the wider economy.
- Understand the fundamentals of a stock with a specific focus on the economics of the business (capital and return)
- Assess what the market is pricing and define whether in your view this presents upside or not, given everything else that you know
- Ignore the noise but be careful to identify structural changes in the business
- Live with your choices

Having normalised accounts, investors will not need to pay particular attention to any specific market or sector factor as there is a fundamental characteristic common to all stocks: capital and return. They provide an excellent basis for a discretionary investment process built upon a core analysis. In the remaining part of this chapter, I will not run a full-fledged review of any business, I instead focus on the drivers of valuation.

The discount rate – the dark side of valuation

I start by analysing the discount rate, the bogeyman of analysts, the dark side of valuation. There is no obscure force at play (although at times it may feel that way). I call it the dark side because (1) this is something that most analysts and textbooks ignore, (2) it is under-researched and (3) it is rarely taught in university programs. Still, it has historically had a significant impact on valuation and the economic cycle.

How to think about the discount rate

The best way to think about the discount rate is to consider the rate of return that investors wish to earn when they provide capital at risk. Every investor has her own view about the desired rate of return, but what matters is the collective number defined by the return expectations of millions of equity investors.

We estimate the discount rate by solving the valuation function for it. There are three components in a valuation function: (1) price, (2) earnings and (3) discount rate. We normally solve for the price, but if you have the price and an estimate of the earnings into perpetuity,[1] then you can also estimate the discount rate. The estimated value is effectively the rate of return that investors expect when providing capital at risk. It is what an investor

---

1. Companies are not a perpetuity but the equity market is. There is a continuous regeneration in listed companies and collectively over the past 100 years they have delivered earnings growth just below nominal GDP growth. By assuming similar long-term growth and similar cyclical patterns, it is possible to build a reliable estimate of the behaviour of earnings to perpetuity, which is then used to estimate the discount rate.

receives over the long term by buying the equity market in its entirety. Figs. 4.3 and 4.4 show the weekly series that we have calculated for the discount rate of nonfinancials and of banks.

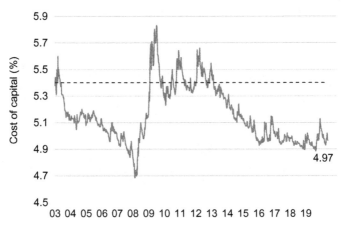

FIGURE 4.3 Discount rate of non financials. *Data from DWS and CROCI.*

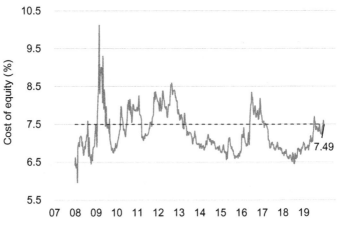

FIGURE 4.4 Discount rate of banks. *Data from DWS and CROCI.*

There is a correspondence between what investors expect and what companies deliver on their operational capital, as we saw for banks in Chapter 3, The analytical idiosyncrasies of banks. For nonfinancials, Cash Return on Capital Invested (CROCI) has had an average discount rate of 5.2% since 1989, below the long-term average of 5.4%. By comparing the current rate with the normal rate, I can then assess whether the market valuation is attractive or expensive.

How the discount rate defines the market level and its changes

The level of the equity market is defined by earnings and the discount rate. Think of a stock delivering 100 into perpetuity, its fair price is 2000 with a discount rate of 5%, 2500 with a discount rate of 4%, 3333 with a discount rate of 3% and 1667 with a discount rate of 6%.

Changes in the discount rate can have a significant impact on the share price. It may sound irrational, but market dynamics are driven by changes in investors' risk appetite. If investors collectively decide to decrease their demanded rate of return from 5% to 4%, the equity markets will rise by 25%. This may happen as investors become bullish and believe in super-cycles (such as the TMT bubble of 2000). The opposite takes place when investors become bearish, as they did in 2009. On 10 March 2009, we published a report called 'Counting the Cost', where we stated that 'The fall in global equity markets has pushed the cost of capital to 5.85% ..., well above the long run return from equities of 5.4%. Our work suggests that as much as four-fifths of the downward move in equity markets since December 2007 is explained by a rebuilding of the risk premium; only one-fifth being explained by changes in earnings expectations.' At the time, in the midst of a perceived great depression, there was a strong impression that profitability would be structurally impaired. As a result, we simulated a situation where the earnings would structurally fall. Even with this strong assumption, we still found that a large part of the market move came from changes in the risk profile. With hindsight I can see that profitability was not affected and, as the earnings chart of the US market shows, earnings quickly recovered. In the end, it turned out that the entire market move was due to changes in risk appetite. Understanding the discount rate and its impact on prices and valuations at both stock and market level is critical to any investment process.

How changes in the discount rate affect the economy

Permanent changes in the discount rate eventually have an impact on the economy. If the discount rate is 6% and investors are willing to accept a lower rate of return to provide capital at risk, 5% say, this suggests that there is meaningful procyclical economic growth taking place. As the discount rate comes down, the benchmark for measuring the viability of investments also falls. More investment projects create value and this fuels greater economic growth, which may in turn lead to a further feel-good factor, increasing risk appetite and investment. Eventually capital is allocated to very high risk projects (Ponzi schemes). When such schemes are discovered, then a reversal takes place. Risk appetite comes down, leading to lower equity prices, lower risk appetite, higher hurdle rates for investments and finally economic recessions.

Earnings isolines

To understand the relationship between prices, earnings and discount rates, I have constructed earnings isolines that show how prices change, assuming constant earnings and varying discount rates. Fig 4.5 shows the relation between price and discount rate for a constant given level of earnings. Given a constant level of earnings to perpetuity, the price becomes a function of changes in the discount rate. This is useful for analysing what happens to price when there is a change in the discount rate, driven for example by changes in risk appetite. This also helps understanding the potential expected rate of return of different companies with similar level of earnings but different prices. The impact on equity prices of a 100bps change in the discount rate is not linear. The lower the starting point, the larger is the impact. Fig 4.6 shows how a full percentage point increase in the discount rate would mean 29% and 11% fall in market values of companies A and B. In the first case the starting point is 2.5%, in the second case, it is 8%. A structural change in earnings is more complex to analyse (Fig. 4.7) as there may be a concomitant change in the level of earnings and in the discount rate that investors wish to attach to those earnings. This is why most investors struggle with equities, i.e. you have two factors that change at the same time. I provide an example that should help the reader that face such situations. In this example, a structural change in earnings should move the stock from Curve 1 to Curve 2. The new price should be 20% higher at 2400. However, there can be situations where the price does not change because of the concomitant change in the discount rate. In this specific case from point A to point C, via point B. In the last

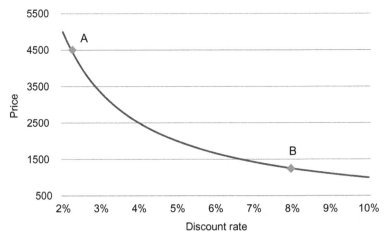

FIGURE 4.5 The relation between price and discount rate given constant earnings. *From the author.*

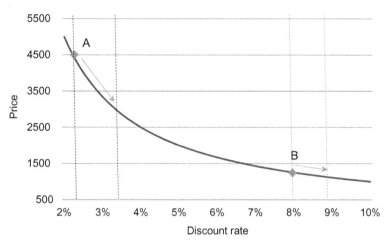

FIGURE 4.6 Larger price changes occur when the discount rate falls to low levels. *From the author.*

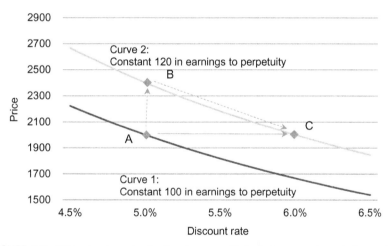

FIGURE 4.7 When earnings structurally change, multiple factors may impact share price. *From the author.*

example (Fig. 4.8), I draw different isolines for different level of earnings. The reader will note that the distance between lines varies, it is significant when the discount rate is small and it is small when the discount rate is high. This tells us that for companies with different level of earnings, there are small differences in absolute prices when the discount rate is high. Conversely there are high absolute differences in prices when the discount rate is low.

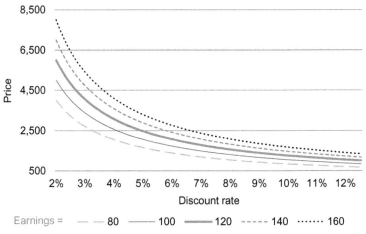

FIGURE 4.8 Earnings isolines. *From the author.*

At a practical level:

- Given a specific level of earnings, changes in the discount rate have a non-linear impact on prices.
- Two companies can have the same price despite different levels of earnings, implying that investors have different return expectations.
- A change in the level of earnings need not change the price. A concomitant change in the discount rate can neutralise the earnings effect.
- Movements in the discount rate can cause price fluctuations, despite no change in earnings expectations.

It is not easy to make sense of market dynamics in a market where both the discount rate and earnings are simultaneously changing, but it is essential to grasp the relevance of the discount factor.

> Tenet #9 of our investment framework: it is essential to understand the impact of the discount rate.

There are situations where earnings do not change and the fall in the share price is uniquely driven by fear, and these present great opportunities for long-term investors.

The bright side of valuation

The bright side of valuation is domain of most research analysts. Their focus is on estimating earnings and deriving a price. Instead, I suggest an approach based on estimating the type of earnings-scenario embedded in the share price and assess whether it is realistic. The four steps of such an approach are:

1. Review the company's earnings and what the market is pricing given the expected rate of return.
2. Analyse the drivers of earnings (capital and returns).
3. Understand how the market has historically valued the company.
4. Assess your assumptions with regard to capital and return embedded in the share price.

Step 1: Economic earnings and implied economic earnings

Given a price and a discount rate, one can estimate the average level of earnings that market is pricing into perpetuity, or over whatever set period is of interest. In this example, I assume the company is a perpetuity, hence Implied Earnings = Enterprise Value/Discount Rate.

Fig. 4.9 compares, in today's money, the real level of economic earnings that the company has been able to deliver in the past (bars) with the level of economic earnings priced by the market to perpetuity (diamond on the top right). In this case, the market is paying north of 10,000 and the company is estimated to deliver around 8000 in 2019 (given a discount rate of 5.15%), This is 40% higher than what is expected and requires much growth that the company was able to deliver in the past, as when earnings levels doubled between 1989 and 1994. If the company repeats such a feat and manages to sustain the higher earnings, then it would be attractive even if it currently seems expensive. However, economic earnings were under pressure between 2011 and 2017 and were basically unchanged between 2004 and 2017. Will the company be able to reverse the trend?

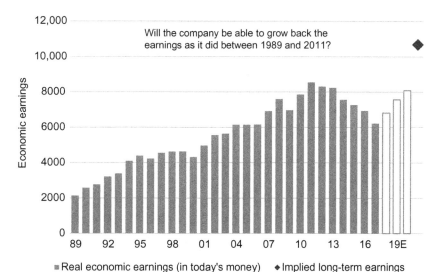

FIGURE 4.9   Economic earnings and implied economic earnings: Coca Cola. *Data from DWS and CROCI.*

Step 2: The drivers of earnings, capital and return

To assess the ability of a company to grow its earnings, I analyse its key drivers, capital and return. Figs. 4.10 and 4.11 explain a great deal about the company.

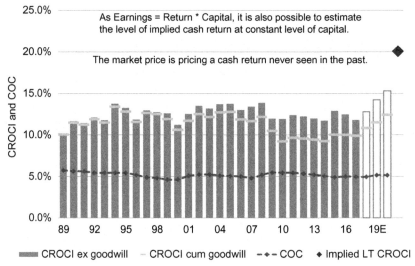

FIGURE 4.10   CROCI cum and ex GW: Coca Cola. *Data from DWS and CROCI.*

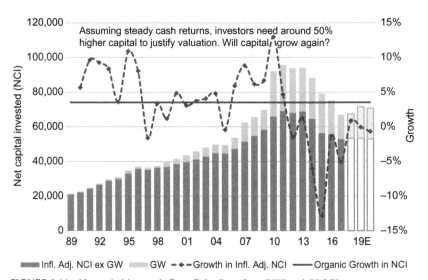

FIGURE 4.11   Net capital invested: Coca Cola. *Data from DWS and CROCI.*

Cash Return on Capital Invested

- There are two measures of cash returns, cum goodwill[2] and ex goodwill. The former provides information about whether the company has been acquisitive, as some companies grow earnings through acquisitions. It shows to what extent acquisitions have diluted returns (Fig. 4.10).
- The little variance in the level of cash returns suggests that this is a very stable business. Other examples later in the chapter portray different types of businesses. As the cash return is above the cost of capital line (the discount rate), I can also see that this business has created value.
- The diamond shown next to the forecast period reflects the level of CROCI that the market currently pricing [Enterprise Value (EV)/Net Capital Invested (NCI) $\times$ CoC], under the assumption of no growth in capital and a 5.15% discount rate.

The Net Capital Invested

- In todays' s money, this chart shows the operating capital invested in the business and its growth rate. Each annual bar in dark measures the absolute value of the NCI excluding goodwill. The amount of goodwill accumulated historically is indicated in clear. The line shows the year-on-year change in the NCI, and its trend over time indicates the growth rate of the business (Fig. 4.11).
- This chart ultimately reveals whether the company is a growth business. Take a retailer with 10 stores and phenomenal growth potential (1000 stores). Its success as a growth company will be measured by its ability to increase store numbers by a factor of 100 without diluting the cash return.

Coca Cola has enjoyed stable and high levels of returns over the very long term, exceeding the cost of capital (dotted line) on average by 2.5 $\times$. Assuming peak returns of 14%, the company needs to attain a 14% annual growth rate in the level of operating capital for a period of 5 years to justify the current price. This may be a challenging assumption given the past growth dynamics in NCI.

Step 3: How the market has valued the company historically
Value/returns analysis

Before concluding the analysis, let us analyse how the market has historically priced Coca Cola. This chart combines fundamentals of the company (capital and return) with market expectations.

---

2. CROCI defines goodwill as the acquisition premium post adjustment for the capitalisation of intangibles.

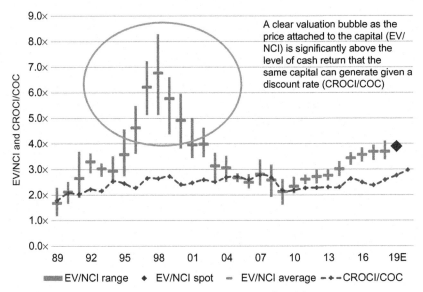

FIGURE 4.12   Value/returns: Coca Cola. *Data from DWS and CROCI.*

Fig. 4.12 contains the four components of the investment process: (1) price, (2) capital, (3) cash return on capital and (4) discount factor. The two operational components are the capital (NCI) and the CROCI. The two financial components are the price (EV) and the discount rate (expected rate of return or cost of capital). Ultimately, valuation converges with profitability and this chart shows that this clearly has been the case over the long term. The company has a stable cash return and has historically delivered between 2 × and 3 × the cost of capital. In equilibrium and in a nogrowth environment, the price of the company ought to be between 2 × and 3 × the capital employed. However, the company has actually traded between 1.5 × and 8.0 × the level of capital.

A company is in bubble valuation when it is 1.5 × above the level war-ranted by its profitability, which means that the stock was in bubble territory between 1995 and 2002 as the stock traded above 3.75 × the level on NCI (1.5 × 2.5). The bubble eventually burst and investors faced several years of negative returns, something I will examine more closely in Chapter 10, Bubbles in equities. The crucial point is that the company has historically traded at a premium, and sometimes its valuation has been irrational.

Despite the company's stable relative returns, between 2 × and 3 × the cost of capital, the market has been very fickle in its valuation. Periods of undervaluation like in 1989 and 2009 were replaced by periods of irrational valuation. In 1998 investors were prepared to pay more than

8.0 × capital for a company returning 2.5 × the discount rate. Irrational valuation began in 1989, but was gone again by 1994. Then came a bigger period of irrationality that peaked in 1998 and took 7 years to disappear. If you thought the stock expensive in 2018, just imagine how it seemed in 1998!

Step 4: Estimating upside/downside to fair price

The framework aims to educate investors rather than provide a definitive answer. This is in line with the arguments proposed by Benjamin Graham (the father of Value investing) in his seminal 1949 work (The Intelligent Investor). Investors need to decide if they find assumptions implied in the share price as being attractive or too optimistic. This means estimating:

- the expected return embedded in the current valuation of a stock and
- the impact that changes in capital and/or return are likely to have

Expected return embedded in the current valuation

In the Coca Cola example, 3.12% is the expected return embedded in the price paid, assuming it continues to generate 2018 cash returns (Fig. 4.13).

Stock:	Coca Cola	Price: 250,000**
Facts	Market Value	EV: $207.4bn
	2008 Earnings	2018 Actual earnings: 6.7bn
	Valuation	CROCI PE ratio 27.4x

EV	Discount rate	Implied level of earnings
207.4	5.15%	10.7bn
207.4	5.00%	10.4bn
207.4	4.00%	8.3bn
207.4	3.12% (Implied)	6.7bn

FIGURE 4.13 Coca Cola: implied and actual earnings given different discount rates. Note (**) I use an imaginary price. This example does not provide an investment recommendation and is for educational purposes. *Data from DWS and CROCI.*

For a 5.15% expected rate of return, Coca Cola needs to deliver 10.7bn of earnings, 59% above 2018 earnings, reflecting consensus' optimism about earnings growth. That said, if the expected rate of return were only 3.12%, then the company is fair value.

At a discount rate of 5.15%, the stock is clearly expensive. Assuming earnings of USD 6.7bn in perpetuity and a 5.15% discount rate, the fair value is USD 130bn. The stock may remain expensive for a long time, but on USD

6.7bn of earnings then the fair value is $P = 6.7\text{bn} \times 5.15\% = \$ 130\text{bn}$. That implies a fall of USD 77.4bn from the value of the company of USD 207bn. Since other stakeholders need to be paid before equity holders − around 3.1bn, in fact − the loss of value for the equity holder would amount to 38%.

Sensitivity analysis

The table in Fig. 4.14 illustrates the different potential scenarios based on changing cash return and growth assumptions for 5 years following this analysis. No fade in profitability is assumed with the company operating to perpetuity.

Growth --> / CROCI	14%	11%	8%	5%	3%	0%
16.0%	14%	3%	−7%	−16%	−21%	−28%
14.0%	−3%	−12%	−20%	−27%	−32%	−38%
12.5%	−16%	−23%	−30%	−36%	−40%	−45%
10.0%	−37%	−42%	−46%	−50%	−53%	−56%

FIGURE 4.14   Upside/downside based on a sustainable level of cash returns and various growth rates over a 5-year period. *Data from DWS and CROCI.*

Conclusions

The approach proposed may not be satisfactory to some but it is a sound starting point for further analysis. The obvious follow-up will be on the business and its future prospects. However, a balanced approach is essential and I invite the reader to reflect on two facts:

- There is a 30-year track record of a company delivering cash returns between $2.0 \times$ and $3.0 \times$ the cost of capital. Much has happened in the past 30 years and the obvious question ought to be: is this time any difference? The focus ought therefore to be strictly on structural issues rather than short-term noise of cyclical matters.
- Assuming the stock is a perpetuity, which is the most bullish assumption that one can take with regard to economic life, only 40% of the stock's value refers to what the company delivers in the next decade. Never lose sight of how little impact the short-term dynamics have on the overall valuation of a stock.

Over the following pages I present some charts with comments as examples of CROCI can be used to analyse different types of stocks (growth, cyclicals and fading) (Figs. 4.15−4.18).

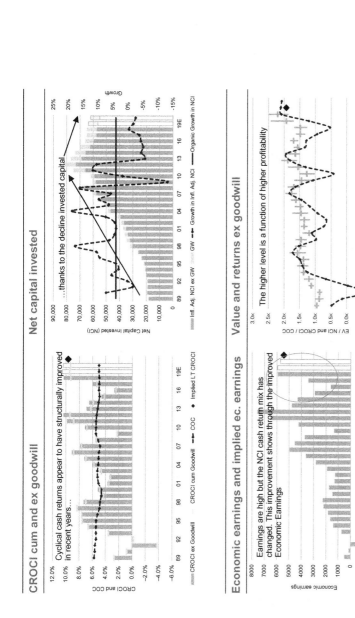

FIGURE 4.15 Caterpillar — cyclical. *Data from DWS and CROCI.*

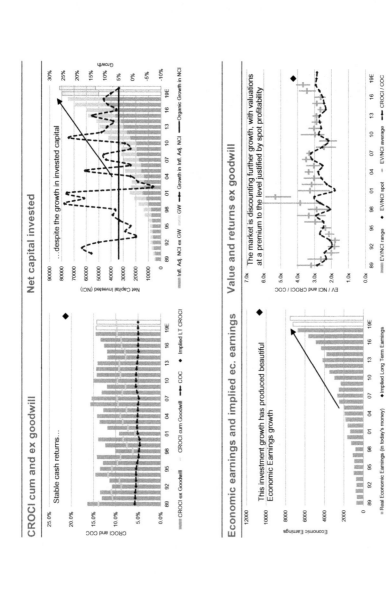

FIGURE 4.16 LVMH – growth. *Data from DWS and CROCI.*

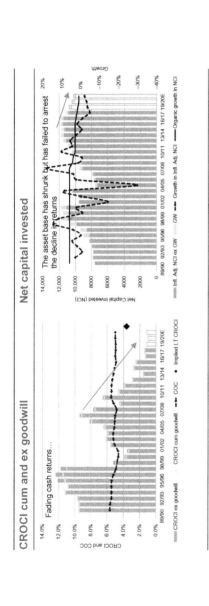

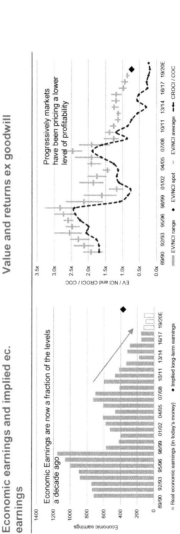

FIGURE 4.17 Marks and Spencer Group — fading. *Data from DWS and CROCI.*

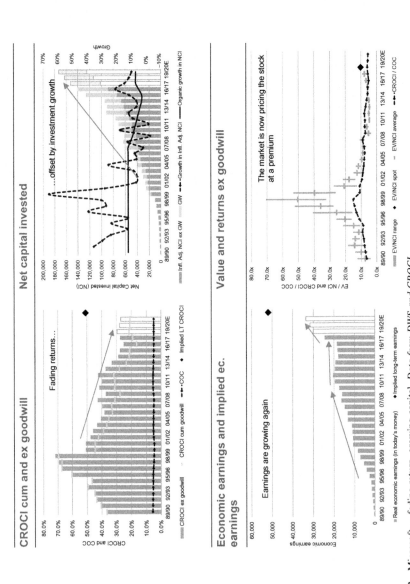

FIGURE 4.18 Microsoft — fading return, growing capital. *Data from DWS and CROCI.*

Section 2

CROCI on investing

To invest successfully over a lifetime does not require a stratospheric IQ, unusual business insights, or inside information. What's needed is a sound intellectual framework for making decisions and the ability to keep emotions from corroding that framework.

Warren Buffett, preface to fourth edition of The Intelligent Investor by Benjamin Graham, originally published in 1973.

Introduction

The world of equity investment has evolved much in the past decades. It has moved from simply investing in single stocks and mutual funds to a more complex world, in which the traditional investment channels have been dwarfed by the rise of ETFs. Changes have been driven by poor performance in the average actively managed fund, its high average cost and the concomitant emergence of low-cost passives. We have witnessed the rise of the systematic analysis of stocks, factors and markets and of quant investing. We have also seen the increased use of certificates and other derivative-based products, giving the consumer the ability to protect capital in exchange for some gains.

Today there is much to be said about investing in equities. But this section will restrict itself to CROCI and how it has been used to define a systematic fundamentally-based investment process. The reader can expect a few stories of how CROCI has been used for stock picking to hold them for a very long period of time, as well as why to avoid certain other stocks. The previous book on CROCI, written by Pascal Costantini, one of the founders of CROCI, provided examples of how CROCI was used in the early days to do single stock analysis for investment purposes, but that does not fall within the scope of this section.

It is not that I no longer believe in stock picking, but rather because there is much to say on the systematic analysis of companies, capital and return as well as of the systematic research in the alpha creation process. The objective of this section is thus to explain how we have used CROCI as a framework for systematic investing[1].

CROCI adjustments to data − is it worth the effort?

Before reviewing how CROCI has been used as an input factor in a systematic investment process, let me share the answer I gave to a client and friend, Daniel Grioli. He asked me: 'can you demonstrate that [CROCI] is worth the effort?' At the time, Daniel was working for a Superannuation Fund in Australia. As a global investor he was keen to use a methodology that would move away from regional and country risk premia to one that would identify the most attractively priced companies regardless of market or sectors. Hence his interest in CROCI. In theory, there should certainly be economic benefits from due diligence process on valuation, but a sceptical investor needs an empirical demonstration that the due diligence process is worth the effort.

Discount rate	5%	5%	5%	5%	5%	5%	5%
ROE	5%	10%	15%	20%	30%	40%	50%
Price to Book ratio	1x	2x	3x	4x	6x	8x	10x
P/E Ratio	20x	20x	20x	20x	20x	20x	20x

FIGURE 1   ROE and P/BV in a perfect market with all companies on a PE of 20.0 ×. *From the author.*

   The demonstration is a straightforward exercise. It concerns the correlation between the drivers of the P/E ratio, that is the P/B ratio and the ROE. If the correlation improves after our due diligence process, then it could be argued that *CROCI is a sounder basis for an investment process and thus worth the effort.* As for what one ought to expect out of this test, there is a perfect correlation between price-to-book and ROE in a perfect market (Fig. 1), where (1) all companies have the same P/E ratio but different RoEs, (2) given the same discount rate and (3) no growth in earnings. A correlation of one means that every company datapoint would sit on the line of best fit when plotted on a chart (P/BV on one side and ROE on the other). In such a market, there is no arbitrage for stock pickers. In practice, a good correlation between the two factors is something to wish for. However, if the correlation

---

1. At the basis of an investment process, there are still a company and an investor; capital and return. The valuation framework presented in the previous chapter is therefore fundamental for any investment process, whether discretionary or systematic. Discretionary investors should make use of chapter four to finalise their investment decisions. The systematic investor will primarily focus on the CROCI data as a potential input factor for investing.

is either too high or too low, then problems result. If the correlation is too high, there is little room for arbitrage because the market is too well priced. A correlation that is too low implies that valuation is not a good discriminator for equities, no better than tossing a coin.

The 2004−18 analysis suggests that the correlation improves on average from 37% to 75% (Fig. 4) when CROCI economic data are used instead of accounting data. Figs. 2 and 3 show the correlation between the price of the

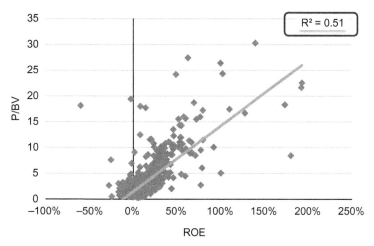

FIGURE 2 2016 Correlation between valuation (P/BV) and profitability (ROE) using accounting data. *Data from DWS and CROCI.*

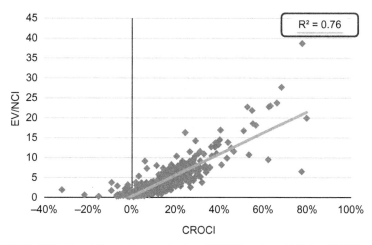

FIGURE 3 2016 Correlation between valuation (EV/NCI) and profitability (CROCI) using CROCI data. *Data from DWS and CROCI.*

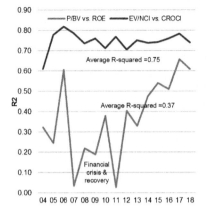

R-squared	P/BV vs. ROE	EV/NCI vs. CROCI
Dec-04	0.32	0.61
Dec-05	0.24	0.78
Dec-06	0.61	0.82
Dec-07	0.03	0.79
Dec-08	0.22	0.74
Dec-09	0.19	0.76
Dec-10	0.38	0.71
Dec-11	0.03	0.77
Dec-12	0.40	0.71
Dec-13	0.33	0.75
Dec-14	0.48	0.74
Dec-15	0.54	0.74
Dec-16	0.51	0.76
Dec-17	0.66	0.78
Dec-18	0.61	0.74
Average	**0.37**	**0.75**

FIGURE 4   Correlation between EV/NCI (adj P/BV) and CROCI (adj ROE) using economic data. *Data from DWS and CROCI.*

assets and their return using accounting and economic data for 2016. This is a visual representation of what to expect when running this exercise.

This demonstration reveals that CROCI provides a sound basis for comparing valuations across sectors and markets. In a world of systematic investing, this is of paramount importance. Accounting-based valuations, on the other hand, use poor accounting data and flawed information, meaning that comparability between different countries and sectors is compromised.

Within this section, there are four chapters. They show how CROCI can serve as the basis for a systematic investment process.

Chapter 5, The performance of economic value, *analyses the performance of economic value* as defined by the CROCI economic Price-to-Earnings ratio. The performance of value, as defined by major index providers and using accounting-based valuation ratios, has been poor over the past decade. I analyse the characteristics of value as presented by the major index providers. I then compare these characteristics to a CROCI-based value methodology that has served as an input factor for investments in funds since 2004.

Ever since the financial crisis, the low level of yield has been an issue for fixed income investors. As I write (June 2019), the 10-year German Bund yield is −0.281% and 10-year US Treasury yield is 2.059%. In their quest for yield, many investors have focused on dividend yield as a proxy for a defensive investment approach. In Chapter 6, Value investing and dividends, I review the risks of looking at high dividend yield as a proxy for value and instead *argue the merits of a method that combines economic value and dividend yield with other factors aimed at removing unnecessary risk.*

In Chapter 7, Diversified investments: CROCI real earnings weighted, *CROCI factors are used as the basis for investing in the entire market.* The weights of companies in major benchmarks tend to be based either on price or on market cap. The rationale is that 'price embeds all important information', that is valuation, growth and risks. This is the view proposed by Efficient Market Hypothesis theorists. Markets are efficient and there is no point in using fundamental factors. This is certainly not the view of the Real Investor who may wish to invest in the entire market. There has been a significant growth in value-weighted indices over the past decade, but they all share the problem of using accounting-based measures to define their weights.

In Chapter 8, Thematic investments – CROCI intellectual capital, I use CROCI to develop a strategy for investing in companies based on intangible assets (Intellectual Capital). Over the past decade, economic growth and equity returns have been driven by companies with apparently little capital and labour. The reality is that such companies do invest in capital, but it is often hidden; it is intangible capital, something that CROCI captures through the capitalisation of intangibles. The growth of companies with little capital and labour has taken place where there has been no real earnings growth at an aggregate level. For equity investors, the implications are significant if these effects are sustained over time. Over 40% of listed equities (including financials) do not have any intangible capital as of 2019, which means that investors are potentially still exposed to a large array of companies with negative real earnings growth.

Chapter 5

The performance of economic value

Chapter Outline

The common perception amongst market participants is that value has had a tough time since the 2009 financial crisis. This is certainly the case if you use traditionally defined accounting measures to define value. Not so using CROCI data, however, notwithstanding a poor 2018. Fig. 5.1 shows the performance of two widely used value benchmarks and Fig. 5.2 illustrates the performance of value based on a CROCI approach. There would have been no broad underperformance on average since 2009 using CROCI,[1] but a whopping 15%−30% using either S&P or MSCI.

---

1. The analysis throughout this chapter excludes financials. Banks were fully added to coverage only in 2018. The ex-Financials analysis adds between 0.8% and 1.1% per annum across S&P500, MSCI World and MSCI EAFE. This is discussed later in the chapter.

Valuing and Investing in Equities. DOI: https://doi.org/10.1016/B978-0-12-813848-9.00005-4
79

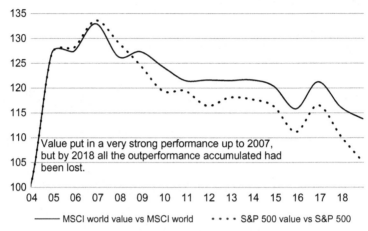

FIGURE 5.1   Conventional measures of value have underperformed the market since 2007. *Data from Bloomberg Finance L.P. Period: 01 January 2004 till 31 December 2018.*

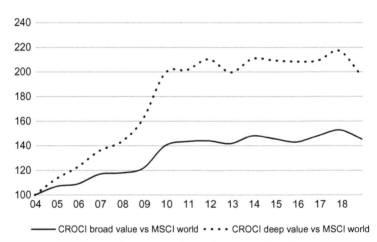

FIGURE 5.2   CROCI economic measures of value have outperformed since 2007. *Data from DWS and CROCI. Period: 01 January 2004 till 31 December 2018.*

How index providers address the concept of value in the market

Various index providers use different approaches to segment markets. The starting point is often similar, that is the sample of stocks that is part of their primary benchmark. They will then create two groups (value and growth) or three groups (value, core and growth) from the sample. Each provider identifies a number of factors to define the constituents of a value or growth index (Fig. 5.3). Once defined, the constituents will be allocated into their 'buckets' according to a relative score and ranking system.

Value factors			
Dow Jones	**MSCI**	**Russell**	**S&P**
- P/E ratio - P/B ratio - DY ratio - Earnings growth (forward based on consensus) - Earnings growth (past) - Revenues growth (past)	- P/B ratio - DY ratio - Earnings per share growth (forward 12 months)	- B/P ratio (the inverse of the P/B ratio)	- P/E ratio - P/B ratio - P/Sales ratio
Growth factors			
Same as for the definition of value	- Growth in forward EPS – long term and short term	- Growth in sales-per-share (past 5 years) - 2 years forward growth as defined by I/B/E/S.	- Growth rate in sales-per-shareover 3 years - Growth rate in EPS over 3 years - Percentage change in share price over 12 months (a measure of momentum)
Overlap between value and growth			
None – Half of the stocks in a benchmark are classified as value and half as growth	Some	Some	Some – there are also 'pure' value and growth indiceswith no overlap

FIGURE 5.3   Factors used by major index providers to define value and growth. *Data from S&P Dow Jones Indices LLP, MSCI, FTSE Russell.*

As an example, S&P standardises growth and value factors that result in a single composite score, which is then used to divide the market into three segments by market cap: value, core and growth. The core group exhibits both value and growth characteristics, hence its constituents appear in both the value and growth index.

The weight of the shared set of companies (core) in either value or growth indices depends on how close each company is to a 'maximum' value/growth score. Russell and MSCI have a similar methodology. S&P also creates pure indices with no companies present in both value and growth at the same time. Dow Jones has gone for a clean cut and, while the scoring system is a continuum, they use a hard cut-off point to differentiate value from growth.

The CROCI approach to value

This is all anathema to the Real Investor, who thinks of value as getting exposure to the companies with the most attractive valuations. The constituents of value benchmarks undermine such expectations as they include:

1. non-value factors (price-to-sales),
2. factors such as *P/BV* that have no reference to the return generated by the capital,
3. non-fundamental measures of value (high dividend yield is not a fundamental measure as dividends can be paid out of debt), and
4. bias based on accounting-based ratios (such as the *P/BV* ratio) that systematically discriminate against specific industries.

CROCI's approach to value is based on the *P/E* ratio. This beautifully simple measure embodies the spirit of what the investor is doing, namely, providing capital and expecting a return. The *P/E* ratio is the synthesis of the investment process, combining the price that the investor pays for the assets (*P/B* ratio) with the profitability of those assets (ROE).

CROCI has two definitions of the *P/E* ratio, the simple economic *P/E* ratio and the risk-adjusted economic *P/E* ratio. The economic *P/E* ratio in its simple form has been an input factor for European-based investments funds[2] since the summer of 2004. It is defined as EV/NCI over CROCI (an economic version of *P/BV* over ROE). The risk-adjusted economic *P/E* also uses the share price volatility of the listed security as a way to incorporate the risk of type B value traps, that is companies that seem cheap but whose earnings may not be sustainable. It is calculated by multiplying the economic *P/E* by the share price volatility of the underlying security. In the United States, risk-adjusted economic *P/E* has served as an input factor for funds since 2015.

Risk-adjusted *P/E* as a measure to adjust for type B value traps

The sustainability of earnings is the perpetual concern of value investors. Throughout section one, I have reviewed in detail the due diligence required for type A value traps, companies that appear to have attractive valuation but revealed by due diligence to be expensive. However, the earlier example of a house perched on a cliff edge (Introduction to section one, *Why valuation is so important for investor*) is a classic type B value trap, attractive but not sustainable over the long term. This second type of value trap is difficult to measure properly.

I discussed in Chapter 4, stock picking based on economic fundamentals, that there is no easy way to embed a fundamental measure in the investment process. The reader may feel that specialised analysts are a good source of

---

2. CROCI first developed three concentrated investment strategy back in 2004 (CROCI EURO, CROCI US and CROCI Japan). The strategies select between 30 and 40 of the cheapest stocks in each region. Each company is equally weighted in the portfolio and held for a quarter. At the end of each quarter the exercise is repeated. The objective is to provide investors exposure to a concentrated portfolio at the value end of the market. There is no cash position in the portfolio. A single factor is used, the economic *P/E* ratio.

information about corporate sustainability. I disagree on the grounds that human judgement is easily clouded by emotion and other biases. These subjective elements can end up removing the most attractive companies from portfolios.

Value tends to be created by a multitude of people falling out of love with a stock and selling it below its intrinsic value. The face of value is normally ugly because the concept of cheap and beautiful tends not to exist in financial markets. A consensus-driven approach risks neglecting real bargains. A company generally needs to have a problem of some sort to be attractively priced.

I have searched, for a long time, for a factor that is emotion-free. Over the years I have taken the view that the share price volatility of the attractively priced security is an effective way of adjusting valuations for the risks attached to the sustainability of earnings. This may seem counter-intuitive, but the logic is straightforward. The price of any company is the net present value of its future expected earnings. High share price volatility means great uncertainty about future earnings. A company that is attractively priced but which experiences violent share price swings is one where the market is uncertain about its long term earnings.

Consider two companies, A and B, with the same share price and earnings. The volatility of their share prices, however, is materially different. Company A's volatility is 60%, but Company B's is only 15%. Both companies are attractive on valuation, but one can assume, all things being equal, that the market has more confidence in sustainability of earnings of company B whose volatility is lower.

Theory and common sense suggest that such risks ought to be embedded in the share price. This is certainly the case in the credit world. A junk-rated stock normally has a higher yield than an investment grade asset and the yield should rise as you move from AAA to BBB rated securities. Modern Portfolio Theory also postulates that an asset with higher risk should compensate investors with a higher expected return (a lower P/E in the case of equities). Under this assumption, the distribution of expected return and risk across the market should resemble Fig. 5.4. However, Fig. 5.5 shows that there is no relationship between valuation and risk; that is risk is not embedded in valuation. At a practical level, this suggests that combining the valuation of each stock with its share price volatility (a kind of Sharpe ratio at the stock level) could be an effective approach to adjusting valuation for the risk attached to the sustainability of the business. Note that companies are not rejected simply because of high volatility. The aim is to ensure that the investor is appropriately rewarded for the underlying risk. If the valuation is appealing given its volatility, the stock is deemed attractively priced.

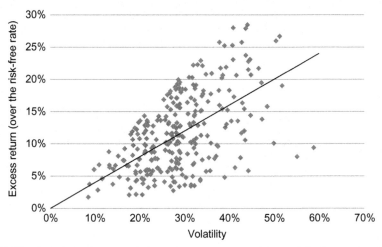

FIGURE 5.4 Relationship between risk and return as suggested by portfolio theory. *Data from DWS and CROCI. The data in this chart is hypothetical and is for illustration only.*

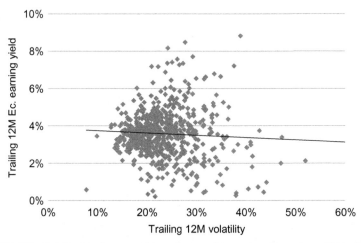

FIGURE 5.5 Relationship between risk and return in practice. *Data from DWS, CROCI, Datastream and Factset Research Systems. The chart shows the relationship between Economic Earnings yield (1/Economic P/E). Companies with negative economic earnings yields are excluded from this analysis. 2015 data.*

A Fama and French test on the performance of value using CROCI data

Having defined the CROCI's value factors, I share the results of a study made by the CROCI team of a Fama and French[3] study using CROCI data.[4]

The conclusions are that both the plain economic *P/E* (Fig. 5.6) and risk-adjusted economic *P/E* (Fig. 5.7) are alpha factors. They generate excess returns over the benchmark over the medium to long term. They are good factors for a value-based investment process. The analysis also suggests that the better the valuation is, the better the resulting performance will be over the long term. A concentrated value approach focusing on the most attractively priced stocks is best.

Plain Ec. PE Deciles	Lowest economic *P/E*								Highest economic *P/E*	
	1	2	3	4	5	6	7	8	9	10
Annualised net total return	11.7%	9.7%	8.9%	7.6%	6.9%	5.2%	5.7%	6.2%	2.7%	2.5%
Volatility	16.0%	15.7%	15.3%	15.5%	15.0%	15.0%	14.4%	15.1%	16.0%	18.5%
Sharpe ratio (RfR: 1.81%)	0.62	0.50	0.46	0.37	0.34	0.23	0.27	0.29	0.06	0.04

FIGURE 5.6 Global developed markets – USD net total returns and volatility of plain economic *P/E* deciles – 2000–18. *Data from DWS and CROCI. Annualised total return shows the compounded annual growth rate (CAGR) of each of the economic P/E deciles between 01 January 2000 and 31 December 2018. Volatility shows the annualised standard deviation of daily log returns between 01 January 2000 and 31 December 2018. Deciles are constructed from the CROCI coverage of developed markets (CROCI coverage of MSCI World Index until 31 December 2017) excluding Financials, by taking semiannual construction of each decile based on descending CROCI economic P/E for each company and calculating equal-weighted returns for each year.*

Risk Adj Ec. PE Deciles	Lowest economic *P/E*								Highest economic *P/E*	
	1	2	3	4	5	6	7	8	9	10
Annualised net total return	12.4%	8.5%	8.8%	8.3%	7.3%	6.2%	6.0%	3.9%	3.2%	2.9%
Volatility	12.5%	13.1%	14.0%	14.2%	15.1%	15.7%	16.2%	17.1%	18.5%	21.0%
Sharpe ratio (RfR: 1.81%)	0.85	0.51	0.50	0.46	0.36	0.28	0.26	0.12	0.08	0.05

FIGURE 5.7 Global developed markets – USD net total returns and volatility of risk-adjusted economic *P/E* by decile – 2000–18. *Data from DWS and CROCI. Annualised total return shows the CAGR of each of the Risk-Adjusted Economic P/E deciles between 01 January 2000 and 31 December 2018. Volatility shows the annualised standard deviation of daily log returns between 01 January 2000 and 31 December 2018. Deciles are constructed from the CROCI coverage of developed markets (CROCI coverage of MSCI World Index until 31 December 2017) excluding Financials, by taking semiannual construction of each decile based on descending risk-adjusted CROCI economic P/E for each company and calculating equal-weighted returns for each year.*

3. See 'The Cross-Section of Expected Stock Returns', published by Eugene F. Fama and Kenneth R. French in The Journal of Finance, Vol. 47, No 2 (June 1992).
4. The following methodology was used to replicate Fama and French research with CROCI data: (a) rank the universe according to valuation as defined by either economic PE or risk adjusted economic PE, (b) break the sample into deciles by valuation, (c) equal weight the stocks in each decile, and (d) run the performance of each decile by keeping the portfolio unchanged for six months.

Efficient market theorists tend to associate the higher return of value stocks with higher operational and financial risk. The analysis shows no meaningful decrease in volatility between the cheaper and the more expensive economic P/E deciles. The Sharpe ratio improves from 0.0 for the highest economic P/E decile to 0.6 for the lowest. The analysis also indicates, with the exception of the first decile, that adding volatility does not improve the return but it certainly improves the Sharpe ratio.

Regional results confirm the strength of the CROCI value factor

At the regional level for the 2004−18 period, the results are consistent with those for Global Developed Markets: Cheaper Economic *P/E* deciles of both US coverage and EAFE coverage generated higher returns without any meaningful increase in volatility from the more expensive Economic *P/E* deciles (Fig. 5.8).

	Lowest economic *P/E*						Highest economic *P/E*			
Deciles	1	2	3	4	5	6	7	8	9	10
United States										
Annualised net total return	11.7%	10.2%	8.3%	9.2%	9.3%	8.7%	10.0%	9.4%	7.7%	8.1%
Volatility	20.7%	19.8%	19.3%	18.6%	17.6%	17.4%	16.4%	16.6%	18.4%	21.4%
Sharpe ratio (RfR: 1.4%)	0.50	0.44	0.36	0.42	0.45	0.42	0.53	0.48	0.34	0.31
EAFE										
Annualised net total return	9.0%	8.2%	7.8%	7.7%	5.3%	7.4%	6.5%	8.5%	8.5%	6.2%
Volatility	18.0%	17.4%	17.2%	17.1%	17.1%	16.5%	16.7%	17.0%	17.4%	16.8%
Sharpe ratio (RfR: 1.4%)	0.42	0.39	0.37	0.37	0.23	0.36	0.30	0.42	0.41	0.29

FIGURE 5.8 United States and EAFE − USD net total returns and volatility of economic *P/E* deciles − 2004−18. *Data from DWS and CROCI. Annualised total return shows the CAGR of each of the economic P/E deciles between 01 January 2004 and 31 December 2018. Volatility shows the annualised standard deviation of daily log returns between 01 January 2004 and 31 December 2018.*

Value investing using CROCI

CROCI is thus a good guide for building a systematic value-based investment process. Two definitions of value can illuminate relative performance versus broader benchmarks. Broad value is the cheapest half of CROCI's coverage universe, whereas deep value looks at the absolute and relative performance of the most attractively priced decile of that coverage. The results indicate that using economic data delivers better performance than accounting-based indices (Fig. 5.9).

	Annualised total return 2004–18	Annualised total return 2009–18
Global Developed Markets vs MSCI World		
Global CROCI deep value	4.8%	3.5%
Global CROCI broad value	2.6%	2.5%
USA vs S&P500		
US CROCI deep value	4.8%	3.5%
US CROCI broad value	2.6%	2.5%
Global Developed Markets ex North America (EAFE) vs MSCI EAFE		
EAFE CROCI deep value	4.3%	NA
EAFE CROCI broad value	2.9%	NA

FIGURE 5.9   Relative performance of deep and broad value in the main regions. *Data from DWS and CROCI. This analysis excludes the financial sector as banks were only added globally in 2018. Not having Financials adds between 0.8% and 1.1% per annum to CROCI over S&P500, MSCI World and MSCI EAFE. The reason for starting in 2004 is that the CROCI team has been collecting as-seen daily data (stored and used for systematic analysis) since then. Such approach removes bias created by ex-post analysis that tends to have surviving bias. Starting the analysis in earlier years (2000, for example), would add a higher level of relative performance to CROCI Value strategies, but results would not be strictly speaking comparable.*

The difference in performance between broad value and concentrated value might relate to relative valuation. The concept of value is simple: if you are expecting a return (let's say 5%) from your investment in equities, by focusing on value you can expect a higher return (let us say 7%). The stronger the focus on value is, the higher the return should be. Fig. 5.10 shows the valuation (measured by economic earnings yield[5]) since 2004 of (1) the market median, (2) CROCI broad value (the cheapest half of the market) and (3) CROCI deep value (the cheapest decile). The average economic earnings yield since 2004 has been 4.8% for the market, 5.9% for CROCI broad value and 8.2% for CROCI deep value. The valuation of CROCI broad value is so close to the valuation of the market as a whole that one has to wonder whether the spread in relative valuation is worth the effort! A focused value approach certainly seems more appropriate.

---

5. The reciprocal of the economic *P/E*.

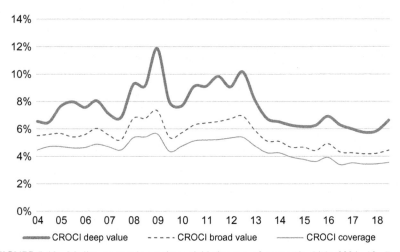

FIGURE 5.10 Median economic earnings yield (inverse of economic *P/E*): 2004−18. *Data from DWS and CROCI.*

CROCI's value approach is markedly different to conventional value

To understand where the differences in performance lie, I compare the operational characteristics and valuation of the 100 most attractively priced companies selected by accounting *P/E*, accounting *P/BV* and economic *P/E* (Fig. 5.11). The overlap between the portfolio of 100 stocks using accounting data to define value and the portfolio based on CROCI data is only 34% (on average) for the period 2004−18. The differences are stark. Compared to the portfolio selected using conventional accounting *P/E* and *P/BV*, CROCI's portfolio of companies with attractive valuations has:

1. higher profitability (CROCI, margins and FCF/sales),
2. lower financial leverage,
3. lower volatility, and
4. significantly more attractive economic valuation measures.

The better quality of the CROCI portfolio (higher profitability and lower debt) helps explain the lower level of volatility than that of the value portfolio built using accounting data.

100 lowest stocks by:	Ac. P/BV	Ac. *P/E*	Ec. *P/E*
Profitability			
CROCI	3.2%	6.6%	9.4%
FCF/sales	2.9%	3.9%	6.5%
Financial leverage			
Total Fin. Lev. / M. Cap	86%	84%	24%
Growth			
Sales growth	1.9%	2.0%	4.4%
Economic Earn. G'th	−1.5%	−2.8%	1.5%
Valuation			
Economic *P/E*	24.6×	18.4×	14.4×
Accounting *P/E*	9.8×	7.0×	9.2×

FIGURE 5.11   Traditional value versus economic value − 2018. *Data from DWS and CROCI.*

There are also significant differences in sector allocation between the CROCI portfolio on the one hand and the accounting portfolios and index providers on the other. Health Care and IT made up 41% and 38% of the lowest economic *P/E* decile at their peaks in 2010 and 2012, respectively (Fig. 5.12). However, their weights fell to 16% and 13% over time − below those of Consumer Discretionary and Industrials, which made up 40% and 21%, respectively, of the cheapest decile at the end of 2018. This is significant different from traditionally defined value indices/products, which tend to be underweight in such sectors.

The picture is similar at the regional level (Fig. 5.13). Europe made up nearly 40% of the lowest economic *P/E* decile at the beginning of 2004 but its weight fell to 24% in 2018. Japan also had a high weight (nearly half of the decile at the beginning of 2008) but its weight had fallen to 33% by 2018. North America had the highest weight in 2016 − close to 60% of the decile − compared to an average of 42% historically (Fig. 5.14).

The high turnover of sectors and regions shows that performance has not historically relied on one or two particular sectors. Instead, sector turnover is the result of bottom-up stock selection driven by changing economic *P/E*s, the same phenomenon that informs the outperformance of Real Value.

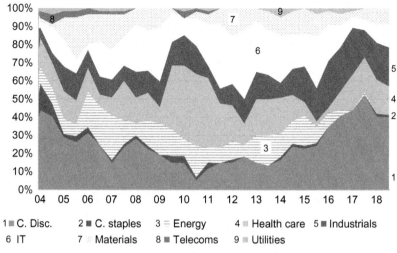

FIGURE 5.12 CROCI deep value sector exposure. *Data from DWS and CROCI.*

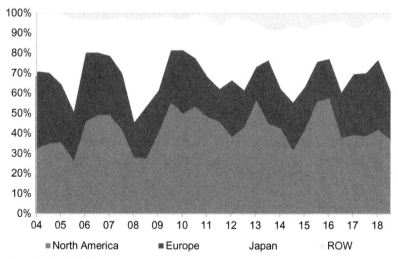

FIGURE 5.13 CROCI deep value regional exposure. *Data from DWS and CROCI.*

	2018	04-18 Max	04-18 Min	Average
Consumer discretionary	40%	52%	5%	26%
Consumer staples	1%	15%	0%	3%
Energy	0%	25%	0%	12%
Health care	16%	41%	3%	18%
Industrials	21%	26%	5%	14%
Information technology	13%	38%	3%	18%
Materials	9%	23%	0%	10%
Telco	0%	5%	0%	3%
Utilities	0%	5%	0%	2%
North America	37%	58%	26%	42%
Europe	24%	38%	16%	26%
Japan	33%	51%	15%	28%
Rest of the World (ROW)	6%	8%	0%	4%

FIGURE 5.14   Sector and region weights for a CROCI based deep value investment approach. *Data from DWS and CROCI.*

The risks of concentrated value investment strategies

There is no such a thing as a free lunch. If concentrated value approaches deliver the best performance over the long term, there are clear risks in specific years. In 2010 and 2018 concentrated value strategies had poor relative performances (Fig. 5.15). The variance in performance is a significant issue. If you are a Real Investor with a long term view, you may decide to ignore it because:

1. the face of value is ugly but you have done your due diligence at the stock level and have already removed any stock that has failed the due diligence process,
2. you do not believe that you are able to identify the most attractive stocks in a discretionary fashion, which is why you are running a systematic approach,
3. some years turn out to be an *annus horribilis*, but you also have exceptional years and you cannot identify a clear trend in the performance, and
4. you are a fundamental investor seeking value.

It certainly all sounds sensible. However, experience suggests that it is easier said than done. It is difficult for most investors to keep the faith when the market is up 20% and your portfolio is only up 10%.

	Lowest Eco P/E									Highest Eco P/E
Year	Decile = 1	Decile = 2	Decile = 3	Decile = 4	Decile = 5	Decile = 6	Decile = 7	Decile = 8	Decile = 9	Decile =10
2000	12.4%	14.7%	10.7%	11.0%	9.5%	–13.2%	–3.3%	–4.6%	–21.3%	–26.4%
2001	7.8%	1.3%	0.2%	–1.4%	–12.7%	–9.9%	–13.8%	–17.8%	–14.1%	–28.6%
2002	2.5%	–2.1%	–4.0%	–8.2%	–9.5%	–15.2%	–12.7%	–14.7%	–22.7%	–27.5%
2003	52.8%	52.0%	43.8%	31.6%	33.6%	27.6%	28.4%	39.8%	29.0%	49.1%
2004	32.1%	22.6%	25.2%	17.9%	20.0%	15.7%	16.1%	14.3%	9.7%	14.0%
2005	19.0%	10.6%	9.4%	7.4%	9.1%	6.9%	7.6%	10.6%	4.6%	8.2%
2006	28.8%	29.0%	30.0%	26.4%	22.5%	22.1%	25.4%	19.7%	18.5%	10.1%
2007	13.5%	9.7%	8.8%	10.2%	6.5%	8.6%	8.7%	7.9%	7.1%	11.8%
2008	–34.9%	–39.2%	–38.1%	–43.1%	–38.1%	–34.1%	–36.1%	–32.7%	–33.8%	–34.6%
2009	55.9%	45.9%	43.4%	45.2%	37.3%	41.2%	28.8%	32.8%	29.3%	32.4%
2010	13.0%	14.1%	14.7%	14.8%	16.7%	16.8%	18.0%	20.6%	16.9%	19.8%
2011	–2.4%	–7.2%	–4.4%	–8.2%	3.0%	–2.6%	–7.7%	–2.2%	–4.6%	–16.2%
2012	10.3%	11.6%	18.7%	13.7%	13.4%	11.3%	21.5%	20.2%	16.4%	18.4%
2013	33.3%	30.4%	32.0%	35.7%	27.4%	29.1%	26.0%	26.0%	27.3%	32.7%
2014	6.0%	5.1%	0.7%	4.1%	1.5%	10.2%	6.9%	7.9%	9.7%	–2.2%
2015	–4.6%	–3.9%	–5.8%	2.2%	–3.2%	–0.5%	2.5%	7.7%	2.5%	2.3%
2016	6.8%	15.5%	9.2%	8.3%	13.3%	3.6%	6.2%	–1.9%	–2.1%	25.7%
2017	28.4%	26.5%	23.7%	27.2%	21.7%	20.1%	22.3%	23.3%	16.9%	25.7%
2018	–17.8%	–12.8%	–12.2%	–11.7%	–10.6%	–8.4%	–7.6%	–7.8%	–7.3%	–5.7%
CAGR[1]	11.7%	9.7%	8.9%	7.6%	6.9%	5.2%	5.7%	6.2%	2.7%	2.5%

Average volatility by decile between Dec 1999 and Dec 2018

Decile = 1	Decile = 2	Decile = 3	Decile = 4	Decile = 5	Decile = 6	Decile = 7	Decile = 8	Decile = 9	Decile =10
16.0%	15.7%	15.3%	15.5%	15.0%	15.0%	14.4%	15.1%	16.0%	18.5%

FIGURE 5.15 Annual returns of deciles clustering companies on the basis of economic *P/E*. Data from DWS and CROCI.

Investment and portfolio construction

The obvious question is whether a different strategy can address performance variance in a concentrated value approach. Inevitably one must focus on two issues: (1) portfolio construction and (2) how much a benchmark should affect stock choices and weights. Other factors can help smooth the market behaviour path of relative performance versus the rest of the market.

Our approach is beautifully simple in its choice of factor, holding period and weighting mechanism. The investor buys a fixed number of stocks. They are the most attractively priced securities. She holds them for a fixed period of time with the same weight. She reviews the process on a regular basis. However, the investor eventually poses questions about whether one ought to use equal or variable weightings, how to define the weight, the size of the portfolio and whether to include other factors. The investor is right about the importance of such matters. I recently came back from a conference organised by some colleagues in Chicago. I was part of a panel where DWS systematic investments were presented, namely, the CROCI approach, Passive ETFs and Quant. All were considered Active investments as there is an active analysis at the source, the primary differences being (1) the relevance of the benchmark in the respective strategies and (2) the data used.

In both Passive and Quant strategies, the benchmark assumes primary importance; that is *where* you get to and *how* you get there are the primary considerations. These approaches were developed to beat the benchmark, a race where all participant are on the same track. The benchmark is analysed in granular detail to develop an investment strategy that can surpass the benchmark. Once the parameters are defined (volatility, tracking error, etc.), you are off to the races. Within the CROCI team, we do have investment strategies that follow such an approach. We also have investment strategies that ignore the path altogether, the *how* you get there. It is the final result that matters. We call this the CROCI *à la Buffett* approach.

The CROCI 'à la Buffett' approach to systematic investing

The *à la Buffett* approach is fully unconstrained by the weights of benchmarks. It is inspired by the principles of Warren Buffett, but it's systematic in nature. I call it the *à la Buffett* approach as Mr Buffett and his colleagues buy value wherever they find it. If they see value in a sector, a market or a stock, they do not look at the benchmark or worry about relative positioning. They follow the conviction of their ideas, believing that over the long term their strategy will deliver the best return. The reference points are the Real Investor and the maximisation of value with as few constraints as possible. Why bother with sector constraints or benchmarks?

Since 2004 CROCI has been used as an input factor to run three concentrated investment strategies (with real money invested) for the three main geographic regions. The strategies buy the 30/40 cheapest stocks in the market, keep them for a period of time and then repeat the process. They ignore the concepts of benchmark, tracking error, efficient frontier and the underlying volatility of the portfolio as well as industry concentration. The role of the PM in this approach is simply to be an intelligent implementer, not to intervene; that is to 'trust' the system. The objectives are the maximisation of the long term return on the portfolio under the following framework. First, due diligence regularly ensures the proper valuation of capital, return and profitability. Second, the concept of limiting concentration is fundamentally opposed to the concept of maximisation of returns. If there is significant value in a sector, you should seek it out. This is what true investors à la B Graham or W Buffet would do. Third, the investor should not care about the market or implement constraints to mimic the market. This approach may raise a few eyebrows but I have learnt to trust it. Since 2004 it has guided real portfolios with these results (Fig. 5.16).

CROCI US $	8.88%	S&P 500 NTR	6.98%	S&P 500 Value NTR	5.95%
CROCI Japan ¥	5.84%	Topix 100 TR	3.41%	MSCI Japan Value NTR	4.80%
CROCI Euro €	7.31%	EuroStoxx50 NTR	3.30%	MSCI EMU Value NTR	3.33%

FIGURE 5.16 Compounded annual growth rates (CAGRs) for CROCI investment strategies since their launch in 2004. *Data from DWS and CROCI. Period: 2 February 2004 till 31 December 2018.*

The CROCI systematic benchmark aware approach

CROCI also manages portfolios that are benchmark aware. These portfolios typically hold 30−50 attractively valued stocks, although they need not be the most attractive. The selection process ensures that the final portfolios avoid style and sector drifts versus the benchmarks that investors may not desire. This may affect both the choice of stocks and their relative weights. The resulting portfolio has a similar valuation to the original unconstrained approach without taking more risk relative to the benchmark than necessary.

For example, assume your portfolio has too many small caps, because you find value in small caps. This overweighting creates a portfolio that is very different from the benchmark, excluding most of the megacaps. In fact, if you only have two megacaps in your portfolio out of total 30 stocks, and each stock is equally weighted, then you are underweight the size factor. If megacaps outperform the market, you lag. You can either ignore this potential problem or you can attempt to 'neutralise' the size factor, possibly by increasing the weight of the two large stocks (and concomitantly reducing the weight of the small caps). Alternatively you can look for other large-cap stocks which have only just missed out on the top 30 and replace a few of the small-cap stocks with these. The aim in this example is to build a portfolio whose overall valuation is as similar as possible to the original 'Top 30', but without taking an unnecessary small-cap bet.

À la Buffett or benchmark aware?

There are fundamental differences between the two approaches. The *à la Buffett* approach corresponds to typology one of investors. It just looks at price and value. The benchmark aware approach buys stocks with awareness of the benchmark, that is typology two. This is a matter of preference, but the investor must then live with the consequences of her choice.

As an analyst trained in fundamentals, I love the transparency of the *à la Buffett* approach, and there is enough performance data to confirm the merits of such an approach. However, our research also suggests that a concentrated value approach yields a better risk-adjusted performance because it removes residual risks vis-à-vis the major index. The price that investors pay is one of transparency in portfolio construction, as it may not always be evident why a stock enters the portfolio.

Chapter 6

Value investing and dividends*

Chapter Outline

As I review this chapter (July 2019), 10-year Treasuries are at 2% and the 10-year German bund is at -0.35%. In the past decade, the low-yield environment has pushed some investors towards high dividend yield equity investments. Dividend is the tangible return component of an equity investment. Defensive high-yield investment strategies are also seen by some as possible replacements for fixed income strategies. Yield is therefore a factor widely used by index providers. But there are many hidden risks in using high dividends as the basis for an investment. It is certainly a mistake to think of single-factor high dividend strategies as value strategies.

Dividend is an important component of your total equity return

Dividends obviously provide an important component of total equity return. In recent years, double digit equity returns have meant that price has played a much more important role than usual in equity returns. But between 2000 and 2018 as much of the total return came from dividends as from price increases (Fig. 6.1).

---

* CROCI launched its dividend focused investment strategies in 2012 (Global, US) and within this chapter I share the insights gathered from our research on the matter. An appropriate dividend investment is based on combining economic value and dividend and remove of some of the risks related to the sustainability of the dividend.

Valuing and Investing in Equities. DOI: https://doi.org/10.1016/B978-0-12-813848-9.00006-6
          95

FIGURE 6.1 Dividends (DR) and prices (PR) contributed equally to equity returns in the past 10 years. The chart shows the contribution of price and dividends to the returns from the MSCI World Index. Data between 1 January 2000 and 31 December 2018. *Data from MSCI Inc. and Bloomberg Finance L.P.*

Dividends ought to be important in a low-growth environment

In a low-growth context, dividends provide a large part of equity returns. Earnings growth is normally capped by GDP growth (Fig. 6.2), and there is reason to believe that trend GDP growth is decreasing. There are many challenges. High debt levels are generally associated with slowing GDP growth. The past few decades have seen a significant increase in the levels of debt (corporate, government and private) cutting out future potential sources of funding. Furthermore, as the interest component of income rises (because of higher debt), less money is available for investments. An ageing population, with more people enter the nonproductive stage of their lives, can cap GDP growth. In a world of low growth, there are two scenarios for equities: a bubble (certainly possible) or low growth.

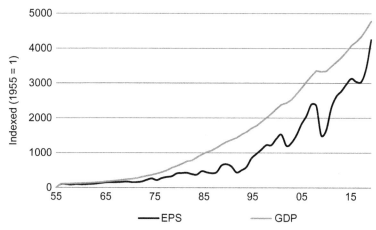

FIGURE 6.2 US nominal GDP versus S&P500 nominal EPS − 1955−2018. *Data from, S&P, Bureau of Economic Analysis and Bloomberg Finance L.P. EPS data shows the trailing 12 months EPS of the S&P 500 Index.*

High dividend yield strategies do not give exposure to attractively valued stocks

In a world of no yield and low growth, following a high dividend yield strategy is understandable. However, it would be wrong to think that high dividend yield provides exposure to value. In a 2012 report[1] to launch a suite of CROCI dividend-focused investment strategies, we found that there was little overlap between the 50 cheapest and 50 highest yielding stocks using economic P/E, accounting P/E and dividend yield (Figs. 6.3 and 6.4).

Overlaps between	Stocks	Ratio (%)
Economic *P/E* with accounting *P/E*	16	32
Economic *P/E* with dividend yield	2	4
Accounting *P/E* with dividend yield	13	26

FIGURE 6.3 Overlap between 3 value focused portfolios of 50 stocks using different valuation ratios − 2012. *Data from DWS and CROCI. Data as originally published in CROCI Focus: The Case for Dividends, Deutsche Bank, DWS, May 2012.*

1. CROCI Focus: The Case for Dividends, Deutsche Bank, DWS, May 2012. All rights reserved. Any unauthorised use is prohibited.

EcPE	AcPE	Div Yld
Actelion Ltd.	Anglo American PLC	Altria Group Inc.
Amgen Inc.	AstraZeneca PLC	Amcor Ltd.
Anglo American PLC	BAE Systems PLC	AstraZeneca PLC
Applied Materials Inc.	Best Buy Co. Inc.	AT&T Inc.
Asahi Glass Co. Ltd.	BP PLC	BAE Systems PLC
Asahi Kasei Corp.	Chevron Corp.	Carrefour S.A.
Astellas Pharma Inc.	Computer Sciences Corp.	Cathay Pacific Airways Ltd.
AstraZeneca PLC	Continental AG	Deutsche Lufthansa AG
BP PLC	Corning Inc.	Deutsche Telekom AG
Chevron Corp.	Daimler AG	E.ON AG
Chugai Pharmaceutical Co. Ltd.	Delhaize Group	Electricite de France S.A.
Cisco Systems Inc.	Dell Inc.	ENI S.p.A.
Corning Inc.	Eurasian Natural Res. Corp. PLC	Exelon Corp.
Daiichi Sankyo Co. Ltd.	Fairfax Media Ltd.	Fletcher Building Ltd.
Dell Inc.	Ford Motor Co.	Fortum Oyj
Eli Lilly & Co.	France Telecom	France Telecom
Ericsson LM Shs B	General Motors Co.	Frontier Communications Corp.
Eurasian Natural Res. Corp. PLC	Goodyear Tire & Rubber Co.	GDF Suez S.A.
Forest Laboratories Inc.	Hewlett-Packard Co.	Iberdrola S.A.
Freeport-McMoRan Copper & Gold Inc.	Itochu Corp.	Koninklijke KPN N.V.
Halliburton Co.	JX Holdings Inc.	Lagardere S.C.A.
Hasbro Inc.	Koninklijke KPN N.V.	National Grid PLC
Hewlett-Packard Co.	L-3 Comms Holdings Inc.	Nokia Corp.
Hochtief AG	Marubeni Corp.	Peugeot S.A.
Intel Corp.	Michelin	Pitney Bowes Inc.
KLA-Tencor Corp.	Mitsubishi Corp.	Portugal Telecom SGPS S/A
Kyocera Corp.	Mitsui & Co. Ltd.	Repsol YPF S.A.
L-3 Communications Holdings Inc.	Northrop Grumman Corp.	Reynolds American Inc.
Lanxess AG	OMV AG	RWE AG
Medtronic Inc.	Peugeot S.A.	Singapore Press Holdings Ltd.
Merck & Co Inc	Pitney Bowes Inc.	Sonic Healthcare Ltd.
Nitto Denko Corp.	Portugal Telecom SGPS S/A	Stora Enso Oyj
Novartis AG	Renault S.A.	Swisscom AG
NVIDIA Corp.	Research In Motion Ltd.	TABCorp Holdings Ltd.
OMV AG	Rio Tinto PLC	Telecom Corp. of NZ Ltd.
Origin Energy Ltd.	Royal Dutch Shell PLC (CL A)	Telecom Italia S.p.A.
Pfizer Inc.	RWE AG	Telefonica S.A.
Raytheon Co.	Seagate Technology Inc.	Television Francaise 1 S.A.
Research In Motion Ltd.	Smith & Nephew PLC	TeliaSonera AB
Rio Tinto PLC	Sumitomo Corp.	Telstra Corp. Ltd.
Royal Dutch Shell PLC (CL A)	TABCorp Holdings Ltd.	Tohoku Electric Power Co. Inc.
Seagate Technology Inc.	Telecom Italia S.p.A.	Tokyo Electric Power Co. Inc.
SMC Corp.	Telefonica S.A.	Total S.A.
Sumitomo Chemical Co. Ltd.	Total S.A.	Transocean Ltd.
Sumitomo Electric Industries Ltd.	TRW Automotive Holdings Corp.	UPM-Kymmene Oyj
TABCorp Holdings Ltd.	Valero Energy Corp.	Veolia Environnement S.A.
Takeda Pharmaceutical Co. Ltd.	Vivendi	Vivendi
Toyota Industries Corp.	Volkswagen AG (Pfd Non-Vtg)	Vodafone Group PLC
Xstrata PLC	Xerox Corp.	Wesfarmers Ltd.
Yahoo! Inc.	Xstrata PLC	Windstream Corp.

FIGURE 6.4 Fifty cheapest/highest yielding stocks (March 2012). Note: shaded stocks are in all three portfolios. *Data from DWS and CROCI. Data as originally published in CROCI Focus: The Case for Dividends, Deutsche Bank, DWS, May 2012.*

Building an economic approach to a dividend yield strategy

Research done since the original study (2012) suggests a structurally weak relationship between dividend yield and economic value. By using Spearman's rank correlation (Fig. 6.5), in which stocks are ordered according to their dividend yield and economic *P/E*, one can observe a correlation coefficient of less than 0.2. The finding is troubling for equity investors, as it means that *high dividend yield per se cannot be taken as a measure of value*.

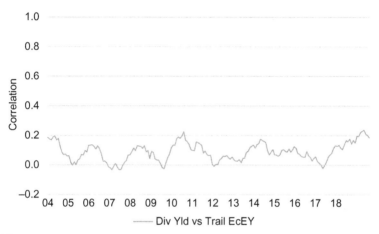

FIGURE 6.5 Correlation between low economic *P/E* and high dividend yield − 2004 − 2018. *Data from DWS and CROCI.*

A further analysis of the operational characteristics of the companies with the highest dividend yields shows:

1. little free-cash-flow after paying dividends, which means there is no buffer to ensure dividends can be paid organically,
2. lower levels of profitability because their businesses do not produce much cash, which is particularly risky if they are also cyclical,
3. no advantage in valuation versus the market; they are not real value stocks, just high dividend payers and
4. high financial leverage, which is another risk in a downturn when the stocks could face both economic and financial troubles.

It is essential for investors looking for yield in equities to connect the distribution of the dividend with the other side of the investment coin, that is the ability of the company to generate earnings capable of paying dividends in a sustainable manner.

The approach that was defined at the time of launching the CROCI based investment strategy was to combine value (economic *P/E*) with yield (dividend yield). At the same time, it was decided to decrease exposure to unnecessary risks, such as

1. low profitability/cash returns (if a company cannot generate a high enough return on capital it will not be able to sustain a dividend to third parties),
2. high financial leverage (leverage may not be a problem in normal conditions, but it could become one in a crisis situation and endanger dividends) and
3. share price volatility (high volatility relative to the market suggests that the market is concerned about the company's risk profile or earnings).

The investment strategy was designed from a fundamental investor's perspective back in 2012. The question was what an investor would expect when looking for a defensive high-yield approach in equities. It was then decided to use a defensive value approach. More research has been conducted since then and our factor-based analysis confirms the desirability of using negative screening when creating a dividend-focused investment strategy. There is no alpha in any of these factors (Fig. 6.6), and they certainly add much unnecessary volatility to the portfolio. With hindsight, the original approach was correct in using these factors to remove the risk — they did not detract from the alpha, but contributed to a better risk-adjusted return (measured through the Sharpe ratio).

	Leverage			Volatility			CROCI		
	CAGR	Vol.	Sharpe	CAGR	Vol.	Sharpe	CAGR	Vol.	Sharpe
F01	9.9%	15.9%	0.54	9.4%	9.8%	0.81	8.5%	14.9%	0.48
F02	10.0%	14.5%	0.59	9.0%	11.2%	0.68	8.5%	15.8%	0.45
F03	7.9%	14.0%	0.47	8.1%	12.5%	0.54	9.2%	14.2%	0.55
F04	7.5%	14.0%	0.44	10.5%	13.2%	0.69	9.8%	13.8%	0.61
F05	9.5%	14.1%	0.57	8.0%	14.2%	0.47	8.7%	14.7%	0.49
F06	9.3%	14.1%	0.56	7.8%	15.0%	0.43	9.5%	14.6%	0.55
F07	7.5%	14.4%	0.43	8.1%	16.1%	0.42	8.5%	14.9%	0.48
F08	7.2%	14.8%	0.39	6.8%	17.0%	0.32	7.8%	14.4%	0.45
F09	8.0%	15.8%	0.42	7.8%	19.1%	0.33	9.1%	15.0%	0.51
F10	8.7%	18.7%	0.39	9.4%	24.4%	0.33	6.1%	18.1%	0.26

FIGURE 6.6 Performance and volatility of leverage, volatility and CROCI by deciles 2004–18. *Data from DWS and CROCI.*

Filter effectiveness

In the original study, a different path was used to assess the effectiveness of the three sustainability filters. The stocks that would have failed the sustainability filters (Fig. 6.9) were compared to what would have been into the actual portfolio (Fig. 6.8). The stocks that would have failed the tests had (1) higher dividend yields, but (2) their dividends were subsequently cut more often and (3) their share prices underperformed in the following 12 months (Fig. 6.7).

	Portfolio	Failed stocks
Dividend cuts	3 over 50	11 over 26
Dividend yield	3.6%	4.3%
Perf. in the following 12m of the portfolio	5.3%	−10.8%
Accounting PE	10.5×	11.8×
Economic PE	12.1×	20.9×
EV/FCF	12.4×	19.2×
CROCI	14%	5%
Financial Leverage	23%	116%
Volatility	17%	21%

FIGURE 6.7 Operational characteristics of stocks failing the tests versus what went in the portfolio. *Data from DWS and CROCI. Data as originally published in CROCI Focus: The Case for Dividends, Deutsche Bank, DWS, May 2012.*

High-yielding stocks that would have failed the original tests were far more likely to cut their dividends than those that would have made it into the investment strategy. A total of 11 (of 26) of the highest yielding stocks from the excluded list cut their dividends, compared to just 3 from the final 50. This suggests that, although the filters cannot guarantee that a company is not going to cut its dividend, they significantly reduce the probability. In terms of price performance, the stocks that would have failed the tests returned −12% over the following 12 months while the stocks that would have made it in the portfolio had an average return of 3.5% over the same period. Some of the stocks that would have been excluded had high dividend yields and might therefore have hurt the performance of a portfolio had they been selected purely on the basis of dividend yield. The average dividend yield of the final 50 stocks was lower than the average of the stocks that would have failed the tests, but the 'safety net' built into the screening process makes the lower dividend more valuable.

	Name	Div Yld	CROCI	Fin Lev	Vol
	Abbott Labs	3.5%	20.4%	0.20	14%
	Asahi Glass	2.1%	9.2%	0.25	31%
	Astellas Pharma	3.9%	10.6%	−0.16	17%
	AstraZeneca	5.2%	20.3%	0.02	19%
	BAE Systems	5.1%	19.3%	0.90	24%
	BASF	3.5%	8.3%	0.32	25%
	Bayer	2.7%	10.8%	0.33	22%
	BHP Billiton Ltd	2.1%	21.4%	0.05	22%
	Bristol-My. Sq.	4.9%	14.6%	−0.10	18%
	Chevron	2.9%	10.5%	0.04	20%
	ConocoPhillips	2.9%	7.5%	0.32	24%
	Daiichi Sankyo	3.5%	7.2%	−0.17	17%
	DSM	3.0%	5.5%	0.02	23%
X	E.On	6.6%	4.9%	0.98	20%
	Eisai	4.7%	8.8%	0.23	18%
	Eli Lilly	5.6%	14.3%	−0.01	15%
	ENI	5.7%	6.5%	0.64	23%
	Ericsson	2.7%	16.1%	−0.06	28%
	Exelon	4.9%	7.1%	0.83	18%
	Gen. Dynamics	2.2%	21.5%	0.37	24%
	GlaxoSmithKline	5.4%	14.3%	0.27	20%
	Hoya	3.4%	11.5%	−0.12	26%
	Intel	3.0%	17.8%	−0.06	24%
	J & J	3.5%	17.1%	−0.04	13%
	KDDI	2.4%	6.3%	0.39	23%
	Kirin Holdings	2.1%	7.7%	0.61	21%
	KPN	6.4%	11.2%	0.86	15%
	Lockheed Martin	3.3%	16.3%	0.65	18%
	Marathon Oil	2.0%	8.7%	0.26	26%
	Mattel	3.3%	13.8%	0.03	26%
	Medtronic	2.2%	33.1%	0.08	23%
	Merck & Co	4.6%	13.9%	0.04	20%
	Microsoft	2.2%	48.3%	−0.11	22%
	Mitsui & Co	2.1%	8.0%	0.87	30%
x	Nintendo	3.4%	29.7%	−0.42	33%
	Noble Corp	2.1%	5.9%	0.30	34%
	Novartis	4.3%	15.3%	0.18	17%
	Pfizer	3.7%	20.7%	0.08	21%
	R. Dutch Shell	4.8%	6.9%	0.23	20%
	Raytheon	2.8%	23.6%	0.36	21%
	Roche	4.9%	15.7%	0.22	17%
	Sanofi	4.9%	16.1%	0.31	22%
x	Sharp	2.4%	4.4%	0.62	31%
	Shin-Etsu Chem.	2.3%	6.0%	−0.20	28%
	StatoilHydro	4.2%	7.0%	0.24	24%
	Takeda Pharma	4.4%	12.1%	−0.27	14%
	Tokyo Gas	2.6%	4.3%	0.54	14%
	Total	5.4%	7.2%	0.30	22%
	VF Corp	2.5%	20.5%	0.30	25%
	Xilinx	2.0%	29.7%	−0.23	29%

FIGURE 6.8 The 50 stocks that would have appeared in the March 2011 portfolio. Note: Stocks with a cross next to the names cut their dividends between May 2011 and April 2012. *Data from DWS and CROCI. Data as originally published in CROCI Focus: The Case for Dividends, Deutsche Bank, DWS, May 2012.*

	Name	Div Yld	CROCI		Fin Lev		Vol	
x	Alstom SA	3.1%	11.1%		1.08	💥	30%	
	Am. Elec. Power	4.8%	3.9%	💥	1.39	💥	17%	
	ArcMittal	2.0%	4.6%		0.48		36%	💥
	BP	3.8%	7.6%		0.41		37%	💥
	British Telecom	3.7%	2.7%	💥	1.12	💥	30%	
	Centerpoint En.	4.9%	5.3%		1.52	💥	18%	
	Chubu Elec Pwr	2.8%	1.4%	💥	1.85	💥	14%	
	CRH	4.1%	6.6%		0.48		46%	💥
	Daimler	2.8%	3.9%	💥	1.13	💥	31%	
	Deutsche Post DHL	4.9%	12.5%		1.01	💥	23%	
	Deutsche Tel.	7.1%	2.9%	💥	1.24	💥	18%	
	Duke Energy	5.3%	3.6%	💥	0.88		15%	
	EDF	3.8%	3.6%	💥	1.71	💥	22%	
	Entergy Corp.	4.4%	2.9%	💥	1.15	💥	18%	
	Firstenergy	5.7%	3.8%	💥	1.48	💥	19%	
x	France Telecom	9.0%	6.4%		1.07	💥	20%	
x	Frontier Comms	11.0%	3.4%	💥	1.11	💥	25%	
	Frprt-McMoran	2.3%	25.4%		0.06		41%	💥
	Iberdrola	4.6%	6.4%		1.10	💥	30%	
	Itochu	2.0%	8.4%		1.79	💥	27%	
	J.C. Penney	2.2%	7.3%		0.44		42%	💥
	Kansai Elec Pwr	2.8%	2.5%	💥	2.14	💥	13%	
x	Lafarge	2.9%	7.3%		1.15	💥	33%	
	National Grid	6.4%	5.0%		1.14	💥	19%	
x	Nokia	6.5%	8.4%		-0.14		35%	💥
	NTT	3.0%	1.7%	💥	0.84		17%	
	Portugal Tel.	6.9%	4.8%		1.13	💥	34%	
	Progress Energy	5.4%	3.5%	💥	1.26	💥	14%	
	Qwest Comms	4.8%	4.3%		1.19	💥	19%	
	Repsol YPF	3.5%	3.4%	💥	0.67		30%	
x	Ricoh	3.1%	3.9%	💥	0.78		31%	
x	RWE	7.3%	5.1%		1.27	💥	19%	
	Safeway	2.1%	4.1%	💥	1.06	💥	23%	
	Saint-Gobain	3.7%	5.9%		0.65		35%	💥
	Southern	4.7%	3.5%	💥	0.74		13%	
	Sumitomo	2.5%	7.5%		2.50	💥	28%	
x	Sumitomo Met Ind	2.5%	2.8%	💥	1.27	💥	32%	
x	Telecom Italia	5.0%	4.8%		1.78	💥	29%	
x	Tokyo Elec Pwr	2.8%	1.7%	💥	3.16	💥	16%	
	UPM Kymmene	3.7%	2.8%	💥	0.57		33%	
	Veolia	5.5%	4.9%		2.09	💥	26%	
	Xcel Energy	4.1%	3.3%	💥	1.15	💥	15%	

FIGURE 6.9 The stocks that would have failed the sustainable tests in March 2011 and why. Note: the explosive symbol signals that the stock failed the specific test. Stocks with a cross next to the names cut their dividends between May 2011 and April 2012. *Data from DWS and CROCI. Data as originally published in CROCI Focus: The Case for Dividends, Deutsche Bank, DWS, May 2012.*

Performance review, sectors and regional characteristics

This framework has been used as the basis for a number of CROCI based investment strategies in Europe since 2012 and in the United States since 2014. It adds value over the medium to long term while providing investors with a different take on the dividend theme than offered by major index providers who focus on dividends (Fig. 6.10).

	2018	3 yrs	5 yrs	10 yrs		2018	3 yrs	5 yrs	10 yrs
CROCI global dividends	−9.3%	8.0%	3.9%	11.3%	CROCI US dividends	−2.3%	12.3%	8.7%	16.6%
Perf. vs MSCI world	−0.6%	1.8%	−0.7%	1.7%	Perf. vs S&P 500	2.6%	3.7%	0.9%	4.3%
Perf. vs MSCI world High Div	−1.8%	2.0%	0.4%	2.3%	Perf. vs S&P HDY Arist	0.9%	2.2%	0.3%	4.7%

FIGURE 6.10 CROCI global dividends and US dividends − performance analysis in USD − annualised returns. *Data from DWS and CROCI.*

Conclusions

It was certainly a great relief when an approach created back in 2012 based on common sense eventually also proved to be correct using more systematic analysis. This important point highlights our progress from a pure discretionary approach to a systematic approach, always underpinned by fundamental analysis.

In this chapter, we provide other examples of 'what you see is not what you get'. Investors looking for yield are generally looking for value, but they normally do not get it. If they are fixed income investors, they are also looking for safety, which they may not get just focusing on dividend yield. Through the combination of various bottom-up factors, a clear investment strategy can be created to achieve investor requirements.

Chapter 7

Diversified investments: CROCI real earnings weighted*

Chapter Outline

Between 2004 and 2014, the team's primary focus was on the development of concentrated investment strategies involving of 30 to 40 companies. Concentrated portfolios offer exposure to the real value tail of the market. However, CROCI is not just about raw value but about understanding the valuation of companies.

CROCI Real Earnings Weighting (REW) is an alternative weighting methodology developed in 2014 that delivers more diversified equity exposure. I have met, over the years, a number of investors outside the traditional value category, who wanted to invest in equities but thought that price did not contain all the relevant information. CROCI REW is the solution for investors who do not believe that the amount of diversification should be determined only by market cap weighting. It gives investors exposure to the entire coverage universe where the weights are defined on fundamental valuation.

Market cap-weighted indices do not serve Real Investors well

While the origins of equity indices go back to the 19th century, their importance has gathered momentum in the past 50 years. They have gone from

---

* This chapter draws from 'The CROCI Approach to Fundamental Weighting', DWS, November 2014. All rights reserved. Any unauthorised use is prohibited.

Valuing and Investing in Equities. DOI: https://doi.org/10.1016/B978-0-12-813848-9.00007-8

being vague reference points used to benchmark portfolio performance to a growing asset management industry in itself.[1]

Within the world of indexation, market cap weighting is the methodology primarily used to define the weight of companies. The general argument is that price (i.e. market cap) contains all the relevant factors related to the business, its valuation, growth prospects and risks.

The merits of using price and market cap to define a benchmark have been widely argued by the Chicago School and the proponents of the Efficient Market Hypothesis (EMH). However, if you are a Real Investor who follows the path defined by Ben Graham, Warren Buffett, Charles Munger and Philip Fisher, you will not be satisfied with market cap-weighted portfolios nor accept that markets are fully efficient.[2]

A fundamental tenet of the EMH is that there is no difference between price and value, which is why using market weight to define the weights in a portfolio works. A market cap-weighted portfolio necessarily assumes that the market is efficient.

For Real Investors, there is a fundamental difference between value and price. Value is what you get; price is what you pay. Investors will always try to get the highest value by paying the lowest price. Real Investors base their investment decisions purely on value considerations. They are not interested in news and rumours and are sceptical by nature. Real Investors think of buying stocks as taking ownership of a piece of the company. They provide financial capital to a company whose operations will earn a return, which is then either reinvested in the company or given back to the shareholders through dividends or share buy-backs.

The Real Investor and the Efficient Market Hypothesis

Real Investors do not deny that markets are efficient. They believe there must ultimately be a reconciliation between price and value, but they also believe that there are periods when stocks can be mispriced. Time is the bridging factor between the two hypotheses; that is, between the market being efficient when price equals value and market not being efficient when a difference exists between price and value. Investors seek to take advantage of temporary mispricings. This relationship between price and value was considered using the example of Coca Cola in Chapter 4 (Stock picking based on economic fundamentals).

---

1. Peter Bernstein's "Capital Ideas" gives a fascinating description of the birth of benchmark investing; an issue that is also covered by Kate Ancell in "The origin of the First Index Fund" (The University of Chicago Booth School of Business, March 2012).
2. It is fair to say that (cap-weighted) index investing has found an unlikely ally in Warren Buffett as he revealed guidance in his will that 90 per cent of the cash to be left to his wife should go into a very low-cost index fund tracking the S&P 500.

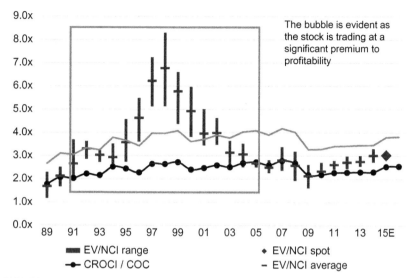

FIGURE 7.1 Coca Cola — economic price-to-book ran vastly ahead of the company's profitability in the 1990s. *Data from DWS and CROCI.*

In a market-weighted portfolio, the weight of Coca Cola would progressively have increased up to 1998 and progressively decreased from 1998 to 2004 (Fig 7.1). A Real Investor interested in acquiring all stocks in the market would have had a lower weight than the one suggested by the market cap, possibly even less than half during peak valuation in 1998.

Fundamental weighting – the challenge is in the implementation

Fundamental indexation is an appropriate approach for investors who:

1. wish to pursue a diversified approach to markets,
2. are sensitive to valuation,
3. wish to have a single solution, still based on valuation, which incorporates different sizes of companies but do not seek exposure to a single investment style (such as value or growth), and
4. do not think that market price captures all the important factors relevant to defining the weight of a stock.

Fundamental weighting is conceptually simple. The difficulty is in its implementation. Which factors should define the weights? How does one deal with growth? Market cap weighting has the advantage of simplicity because the price embeds all the information and the same factor can be used the world over. In 2005, though, the article on "Fundamental Indexation" (Arnott,

Hsu and Moore, Financial Analysts Journal, 2005) sparked a proliferation of alternative weighting schemes and products.

The standard approach to fundamental weighting is to define weights using a multitude of factors. The MSCI USA Value Weighted Index, for example, defines weights based on value criteria. The index weights are determined using fundamental accounting data: sales, book value, earnings and cash earnings. The ultimate company weight is the mean of the four factor weights. However, there are significant limits to a multifactor approach. Equity investors provide financial capital. They do not receive back a ragtag of sales, earnings and book value. No, they receive just earnings, some of which are in the form of dividends and some of which are reinvested in the business to drive price appreciation. Using a multifactor approach for fundamental weighting is rather like saying to an investor, 'if you give me capital, then I will give you a bit of sales, a little of the book value, a bit of profits and a little bit of this and a little bit of that in return'. And that is simply not what happens.

Earnings is the preferred fundamental weighting factor

A fundamentally weighted approach should be linked to the 'investment cycle', where there are only three factors that can rationally be taken into account (1) the book (representing the operating capital), which is how the financial capital is used, (2) the earnings, which is what the shareholder gets as a return for providing financial capital (some of that will go back in the form of dividends, some in the form of capital reinvested) and (3) dividends, for those hard-core investors who believe that any cash reinvested for growth is just 'wasted'. Earnings alone should be considered for fundamental weighting. Earnings is a more comprehensive measure as it includes earnings reinvested in the operations and paid in dividends and excludes companies that pay dividends above the level that is economically justifiable.

Weighting by book (or operating assets) does not give exposure to real value

In Chapter 6, Value investing and dividends, I analysed how dividends do not provide exposure to value. This is also the case for the price-to-book ratio (or book value). Book value has long been used by some value investors and it is relevant to discuss why it should not be considered. Earnings is a more comprehensive fundamental factor than book value as it implicitly contains the earnings power of the book. In the end, earnings are nothing but the result of the book value times the return on equity (book). Using just book value leads to the implicit assumption that all companies and sectors within the market have similar or converging ROEs. This is a strong assumption to make, and Fig. 7.2 shows that it is wrong because cash returns at the

CROCI (cash return) for US sectors	2018E	5-year average	10-year average	20-year average
Information technology	26.4%	24.5%	24.0%	19.7%
Health care	19.2%	18.4%	17.5%	17.6%
Consumer staples	13.7%	12.7%	12.6%	13.1%
Communication services	10.7%	9.1%	8.1%	7.3%
Industrial	10.5%	10.1%	9.9%	9.4%
Consumer discretionary	9.0%	8.5%	8.1%	6.9%
Materials	7.8%	6.8%	6.6%	6.1%
Energy	3.9%	2.6%	4.6%	6.5%
Utilities	3.9%	3.6%	3.8%	3.9%

FIGURE 7.2 Sector profitability is very stable over time. *Data from DWS and CROCI. CROCI cash returns in this table are agglomerated figures for the CROCI coverage universe of US stocks excluding Financials and Real Estate.*

sector level tend to be sticky. Cash returns tend to be very stable over time, the only partial exceptions are IT (gradually rising cash returns, but at already elevated levels) and Energy (temporary increase during the commodity super-cycle. Weighting a portfolio by accounting book value [or even by real operating assets as measured by net capital invested (NCI)] also tends to overweight expensive companies and sectors (such as Telecoms and Utilities) at the expense of cheaper ones (such as Health Care and IT). In our example (Fig 7.3), a portfolio weighted on assets (NCI) would be 39% weighted in Energy, Telecoms and Utilities — asset-intensive sectors with very low profitability. The high-profitability, low Ec PE sectors of Health Care and IT, however, would be a combined 20 percentage points underweight relative to market cap. Finally, the systematic analysis of factors also concludes that there is little value in the EV/NCI as a selection factor.

Fundamental weighting and growth

A fair criticism of a fundamentally weighted approach is that none of the factors used are growth factors, which proponents of the EMH would argue is normally incorporated in market cap weighting since the price ought to embed future growth expectations.

Most fundamental weighting approaches struggle to include a fundamental growth factor. Any factor involving earnings or earnings averages tends to assume that current profitability is constant and that there is no growth differential amongst companies. The implicit assumption is that companies

Sectors	Weight by NCI	Weight by market cap	CROCI (2018E)	EcPE (2018E)
Communication services	13.6%	13.1%	10.7%	26.4
o.w. Telecom Services	8.7%	2.6%	4.9%	27.4
Consumer discretionary	13.8%	13.6%	9.0%	33.1
Consumer staples	7.9%	10.5%	13.7%	27.5
Energy	15.0%	6.1%	3.9%	31.7
Health care	8.6%	14.5%	19.2%	22.7
Industrials	13.1%	10.6%	10.5%	27.7
Information technology	9.2%	24.5%	26.4%	25.0
Materials	4.6%	3.1%	7.8%	27.3
Utilities	14.1%	3.8%	3.9%	28.8
Total	100.0%	100.0%	11.0%	26.6

FIGURE 7.3 Weighting US sectors on book (or NCI) leads to overweights in low profitability sectors and underweights in real value sectors. *NCI*, net capital invested. *Data from DWS and CROCI. Weights as of 31 December 2018, US universe refers to CROCI coverage universe of US stocks excluding Financials and Real Estate.*

with the largest earnings will remain large, whilst newcomers will remain small. Several operators adjust for growth indirectly by including as many small companies as possible. All evidence manifestly points towards higher average growth in smaller companies while bigger companies tend to revert to the mean.

Equal weighting is the most common mean reversion approach in indexation.[3] It is appropriate for small concentrated portfolios, but when applied to benchmarks it implies that all companies will remain economically important in the future, with no economic variations across sectors and markets. Equal weighting penalises sectors such as IT and HC because of their larger average company size, while low average company size results in CD, Materials and Utilities being overweighted.

Partial mean reversion is the most appropriate approach for dealing with growth. It combines the fundamental advantages of a real-earnings-weighted

---

3. Another common argument in favour of equal weighting is that it provides access to a "rebalancing premium", effectively benefiting from reversion of short/mid-term momentum by selling down the portfolio leaders and buying back the portfolio laggards when readjusting the weights. ("Volatility Harvesting: Why Does Diversifying and Rebalancing Create Portfolio Growth?" by Bouchey, Nemtchinov, Paulsen, and Stein, Journal of Wealth Management, Fall 2012).

approach with a partial mean reversion assumption at the sector level. In practice, this is a two-stage approach. First, it estimates the real Equity Earnings of companies and aggregates them at the sector level, defining the sector weights. Second, it applies the mean reversion approach within each sector by defining the weights on the basis of the square root of earnings. This application effectively assumes that over time markets will bring about a normalisation (mean reversion) in the relative size and profitability of companies operating within the same sector. We apply the process at the sector level since the economic structures of sectors tend to differ. For example, Utilities is a much more fragmented sector than Telecoms or Health Care. Applying mean reversion at portfolio level implies that the economic power of Utilities will increase at the expense of Telecoms and Health Care. This is also a significant issue for equal-weighting approaches applied at the market level (Fig. 7.4).

Using the square root of earnings at the sector level assumes that the mean reversion process will take time and may never actually be completed. But crucially it is an intrasector dynamic rather than an intersector one. Some small companies may end up becoming bigger than the larger companies within the sector, but the regular reconstitution of the portfolio will normally adjust for that. The use of the square root to interpolate between a given weighting scheme (Equity Earnings weighting in this case) and equal weighting has been extensively described and analysed in the academic literature: the concept was first employed as "diversity weighting" based on the

Sectors	Equal weight	Market cap weight	Equity earnings weight
Comm. Services	6.1%	13.1%	13.6%
Cons. discretionary	19.1%	13.6%	10.8%
Cons. staples	9.0%	10.5%	10.3%
Energy	7.8%	6.1%	5.3%
Health care	11.0%	14.5%	17.4%
Industrials	16.2%	10.6%	10.6%
Inf. technology	17.1%	24.5%	25.1%
Materials	6.1%	3.1%	3.0%
Utilities	7.2%	3.8%	3.6%

FIGURE 7.4 Equal weighting a broad-market portfolio may tilt exposure away from value. *Data from DWS and CROCI. Weights are for CROCI coverage of US stocks excluding Financials and Real Estate.*

square root of market cap.[4] Weighting by the square root of Equity Earnings (EqE1/2) can be thought of as being halfway between pure Equity Earnings weighting (EqE1) and equal weighting (EqE0).

CROCI equity earnings, the factor for fundamental weighting

CROCI Earnings refers to the total earnings attributable to all providers of financial capital. In defining the fundamental weight of an equity product, only the portion that could accrue to shareholders is considered, called *CROCI Equity Earnings*. It is defined as the part of firm-wide earnings attributable to shareholders, so:

$$\text{Equity Earnings} = \text{Econ. Earnings} \times \frac{\text{Market Cap}}{\text{Enterpr. Value}} = \text{Econ. Earnings Yield} \times \text{Market Cap}$$

This approach creates a value tilt in the portfolio, given that another way of expressing equity earnings is as the product of market cap and economic earnings yield. The higher the earnings yield of a company (good value), the greater the overweight of this company relative to its market cap weight. Conversely a company with a low earnings yield will be underweight in this approach, and the underweight will increase with lower earnings yield.

In a portfolio weighted by equity earnings, a company will be overweight (compared to market cap weighting) if and only if its economic valuation is cheaper than the portfolio's aggregate valuation, and the magnitude of the over/underweight will be proportional to the relative valuation of the company.

In Fig. 7.5, B is both more financially geared and has a less attractive valuation than A. Firm-wide earnings would overweight B relative to market cap (50% vs 40%), whereas CROCI equity earnings underweight B (33% vs 40%), in line with its higher Ec *P/E* ratio.

Company	CROCI earnings	Enterprise value	Market cap	Equity earnings	Ec P/E	Mkt cap weight	Earnings weight	Equity earnings weight
A	50	750	750	50	15.0x	60%	50%	67%
B	50	1000	500	25	20.0x	40%	50%	33%

FIGURE 7.5 Weighting by equity earnings will always tilt towards real value. *Data from DWS and CROCI. For illustrative purposes only, not based on actual company data.*

---

4. For example "A Survey of Alternative Equity Index Strategies" by Chow, Hsu, Kalesnik and Little, Financial Analysts Journal, 2011; and "Portfolio Generating Functions" by Fernholz, 1995.

CROCI Real Earnings Weighting — methodology, operational characteristics and performance

The following are the five stages of the CROCI Real Earnings weithed methodology to investing in equities: (1) Adding companies to the CROCI database—a due diligence process is performed by CROCI analysts, who identify the adjustments required to construct a full economic valuation of companies. Some companies may be discarded at this stage. (2) Estimate the equity earnings attributable to free-float equity holders. (3) Define sector weights based on the total equity earnings of all companies in the same sector. (4) Define the weight of each stock within its sector on the basis of the square root of its equity earnings. (5) Repeat the process twice a year. The analysis of investment strategies based on CROCI REW delivers (1) better exposure to attractive valuations, (2) differences in sector weights (significant overweight in Health Care, IT and Financials), which can be very different in specific periods, (3) lower volatility in the price dynamics of investments and (4) different weights in stocks (Figs 7.6—7.8).

REW outperformed the underlying market-weighted benchmarks in 2004 to 2018. It had a better risk-adjusted return that the market (Sharpe ratio). The worst drawdown was less than that of the market cap-weighted benchmarks (Fig. 7.9).

Sectors	Market cap weight	CROCI REW
Communication services	12.0%	12.0%
Consumer discretionary	12.5%	9.4%
Consumer staples	9.7%	8.9%
Energy	5.6%	4.7%
Financials	8.4%	12.4%
Health care	13.3%	14.2%
Industrials	9.8%	9.5%
Information technology	22.5%	23.2%
Materials	2.8%	2.9%
Utilities	3.5%	2.8%
Total	100.0%	100.0%

FIGURE 7.6 CROCI REW — sector weights comparison. *Data from DWS and CROCI. Portfolio weights as of 31 December 2018.*

FY1 company data, weighted averages	Market cap weight	CROCI REW
Ratios		
Net profit margin	18.5%	18.1%
CROCI	21.0%	20.3%
FCF / sales	15.1%	15.5%
Net Fin. Liabilities / Mkt Cap	25.8%	34.3%
Valuation		
EV/NCI (econ. price to book)	5.82x	5.05x
Economic PE	24.6x	21.7x
Accounting PE	15.7x	13.4x
FCF yield	4.5%	5.2%
Div yield	2.2%	2.3%

FIGURE 7.7 CROCI REW — operational and financial characteristics. *Data from DWS and CROCI. Operational/financial characteristics as of 31 December 2018.*

Market cap weight		CROCI REW	
Microsoft	4.093%	Apple	2.063%
Apple	3.926%	Alphabet	1.832%
Amazon	3.892%	Facebook	1.708%
Alphabet	3.799%	Microsoft	1.526%
Facebook	1.982%	JPMorgan Chase	1.252%
J & J	1.823%	Bank of America	1.155%
JPMorgan Chase & Co	1.762%	Intel	1.124%
Visa Inc	1.577%	AT&T	1.076%
ExxonMobil	1.507%	Wells Fargo	1.022%
Wal-Mart	1.424%	Disney (Walt)	0.973%

FIGURE 7.8 Top 10 holdings in US universe by weighting scheme. *Data from DWS and CROCI. Portfolio weights are based on selection as of 31 December 2018.*

	US All Cap	US Large	US Mid	Int'l USD	World USD	Europe EUR	Japan JPY
Compound annual growth	9.3%	9.1%	11.6%	6.2%	7.9%	7.2%	4.9%
Sharpe ratio	0.59	0.58	0.57	0.32	0.48	0.50	0.28
Main benchmark	S&P 500	S&P 500	S&P 500	MSCI EAFE	MSCI World	MSCI Europe	TOPIX 100
In comparison to benchmark:							
Annual excess return	2.1%	1.9%	4.4%	1.6%	1.8%	2.1%	2.0%
Ann. monthly volatility	Lower	Lower	Higher	Lower	Lower	Lower	Lower
Worst drawdown	Less	Less	Less	Less	Less	Less	Less
Correlation	0.98	0.98	0.90	0.99	0.99	0.97	0.97
Tracking error	2.5%	2.6%	8.0%	2.9%	2.2%	3.5%	4.5%

FIGURE 7.9 Performance of CROCI REW: 2004−2018. *Data from DWS and CROCI, Bloomberg Finance LP. Statistics based on net total returns for the period 19/03/2004−31/12/2018 and all figures are for USD performance unless stated otherwise. Sharpe ratio, volatility, correlation and tracking error based on monthly returns. The CROCI REW Strategies have no operating history prior to 30/09/2014.*

Conclusion

Over the past decade, there has been significant growth in benchmark investing. Any benchmark using either price or market cap, as its primary weighting mechanism, implicitly assumes that markets are efficient, that is there is no difference between price and value. This approach fails to satisfy the requirements of the Real Investor wanting to invest in the broad market.

It is wrong to assume that the Real Investor is interested only in single stocks or concentrated portfolios. As a Real Investor, I certainly do not want to be so limited in my choice of investments.

Many index providers have proposed different approaches for broad value-weighted indices. However, they generally revolve around stated accounting data, an inappropriate investment methodology for the Real Investor. In this chapter, I have presented something more appropriate, using real earnings as the basis for broad-based investment. It ensures that weightings are based on fundamentals, rather than on speculative behaviour. Historical analysis suggests performance is better than that of major benchmarks with lower risk, without significantly differing from pure market cap-weighted indices at any given point.

Appendix

Sector weights and valuation at the peak of the 2000 bubble

While the reader may find little difference in the two approaches, it is worth noticing the differences in weights and valuation (ex Financials) at the peak of the 2000 TMT Bubble (Fig. 7.10). IT was half weighted with significant overweight in Health Care, Staples and Utilities. There was a significant difference in valuation ratios between a market cap-weighted portfolio and a Real Earnings Weighted one. (Fig 7.11).

Sectors	Market cap weight	CROCI REW
Consumer discretionary	10.9%	13.8%
Consumer staples	10.9%	17.0%
Energy	5.6%	4.6%
Health care	11.2%	15.7%
Industrials	9.8%	11.5%
Information technology	43.6%	24.6%
Materials	2.3%	3.6%
Telecoms	4.8%	5.8%
Utilities	1.6%	3.3%
Total	100.0%	100.0%

FIGURE 7.10 US sector weights in March 2000 at height of TMT bubble: significant IT underweight. *Data from DWS and CROCI.*

FY1 company data, weighted averages	Market cap weight	CROCI REW
Ratios		
Net profit margin	15.1%	12.5%
CROCI	20.8%	15.9%
FCF / sales	8.4%	7.3%
Net fin. liabilities / Mkt cap	8.2%	20.1%
Valuation		
EV/NCi (econ. price to book)	19.59x	8.62x
Economic PE	38.7x	26.0x
Accounting PE	29.9x	19.3x
FCF yield	2.2%	3.2%
Div yield	1.0%	1.5%

FIGURE 7.11 US operational and financial characteristics in March 2000. *Data from DWS and CROCI.*

Chapter 8

Thematic investments — CROCI intellectual capital

Chapter Outline

Thematic investing is about investing in an asset that will deliver a better return than the rest of the market, the challenge is not to fall in a speculative trap. I have witnessed several situations where companies have a remote connection to a theme but are still included in a thematic investment. I have also seen companies that deliver high level of revenue growth without comparable earnings growth, because either competitors improved or capital

Valuing and Investing in Equities. DOI: https://doi.org/10.1016/B978-0-12-813848-9.00008-X
     117

requirements grew at a faster pace than revenues. In this chapter, CROCI is used to define an investment process that provides exposure to companies that invest in intellectual capital (intangible capital), whose weight is a function of valuation.

The rising importance of intellectual capital in the investment world

Ideas have always contributed to economic growth, but in the past the relationship between ideas and growth manifested itself through hard assets. Think of railways, shipping, large chemical and steel plants and auto manufacturers. The economics of an idea required significant investment in plant and machinery as well as a substantial amount of labour. Over the past decade, though, economic growth and equity returns have been driven by companies with apparently little capital and labour.[1] The reality is that such companies do invest in capital, but it is often hidden. It is intangible or, better, intellectual capital, something that CROCI captures through the capitalisation of intangibles. The growth of companies with little capital and labour often takes place in a context where there has been no real earnings growth at an aggregate level. For equity investors the implications can be significant if these effects continue. In 2019 over a third of the companies covered in the nonfinancial part of the market lacked intangible capital. This was also the case for Financials, which means that investors are potentially still exposed to two-fifths with either no or negative real earnings growth.

This situation is not new. There is an intrinsic relationship between large investable benchmarks and the economy. As the economy has evolved over the past century, so too has the composition of benchmarks. New companies emerge and others fade away. As an asset class, equities exist in perpetuity, but individual companies do not. They are like the cells of an organism: the organism itself might have a long life, but there is constant change at the cellular level. If the future belongs to companies that are able to deliver economic growth with little physical capital, investors in equity benchmarks can continue to invest in companies whose businesses are structurally challenged by these changes. In a Darwinian survival-of-the-fittest approach, avoiding structural declines becomes fundamental as a strategy for offsetting stagnation. Investors can get exposure to this structural change because companies with intellectual capital now represent a significant part of the listed universe. The challenge is how one ought to get exposure. Buying a specific sector is a possible option, but this is a structural theme that

---

1. The emergence of such trends has attracted more and more attention. For those interested in further reading, I suggest the book written by Haskel & Westlake (2017), *Capitalism Without Capital*. The book offers a comprehensive analysis of the increasing relevance of intangible capital in our life and economies.

underpins the entire economy. Within this chapter, I take the reader down the path that has led to the development of a thematic investment: CROCI intellectual capital.

The new economy is driving growth

Equity markets have performed strongly since the 2009 financial crisis – something of a surprise given lukewarm GDP and earnings growth as a backdrop. The problems of the financial sector are well known, but earnings growth in the rest of the market stalled after 2007 in real terms (Figs 8.1 and 8.2).

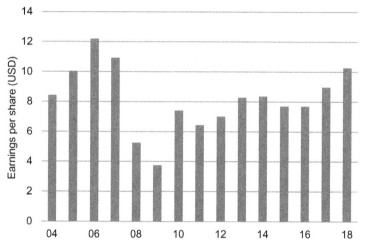

FIGURE 8.1   Financials: 2018 nominal EPS of the MSCI ACWI Financials Index were still below the 2006 level. *Data from Bloomberg Finance L.P.*

This strong market performance can be explained, however, by considering (1) central banks' policies and (2) growth in the IT sector. Central banks' accommodative monetary policies have pushed asset prices beyond the levels earnings could justify. The median economic *P/E* of CROCI's global coverage universe has risen from 22.8× in 2007 to 28.9× in 2018. The role of technology and related companies has been equally important. The strong earnings growth that these companies have delivered in recent years has offset much of the weakness in growth elsewhere. This disconnect between the earnings growth of the IT (and related) companies and the broader market has had IT companies leading the market over recent years. The economic significance of these new economy companies can be observed by their market leadership (Fig. 8.3). In 2007, 4 of the 10 largest companies came from the energy sector. Two of the remainder were telecom companies. Of these six, only Exxon remains in the top 10 today. Only one IT company – Microsoft – appeared in the Top 10 list

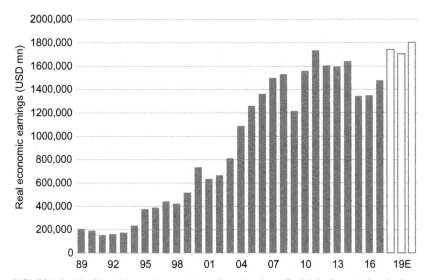

FIGURE 8.2 Nonfinancials: real economic earnings have been flattish in the past decade. *Data from DWS and CROCI.*

Sector	2018		2007		1997	
	# Co	Mkt Cap Wt	# Co	Mkt Cap Wt	# Co	Mkt Cap Wt
C. Services	2	21.0%	2	16.3%	1	7.8%
Discretionary	1	13.8%	–	–	1	7.8%
Staples	1	5.5%	1	8.2%	2	19.6%
Energy	1	6.3%	4	43.9%	2	19.2%
Financials	2	13.0%	1	7.1%	–	–
H. Care	1	7.5%	–	–	1	9.1%
Industrials	–	–	1	13.7%	1	17.1%
IT	2	32.9%	1	10.8%	2	19.3%
Materials	–	–	–	–	–	–
Utilities	–	–	–	–	–	–

FIGURE 8.3 Market leadership changes since 1997: the 10 most highly valued companies in the MSCI World.[2] *Data from DWS and CROCI and MSCI Inc. The table shows sector classification and market cap weights of the 10 largest companies in the MSCI World at the end of 1997, 2007 and 2018.*

in 2007, and the Consumer Discretionary sector had no representatives. By contrast, the top 10 in January 2019 was made up of five IT and related stocks (two of these have since been reclassified as

---

2. The two Communication Services companies that are now part of the ten highly valued companies are both from the Media & Entertainment subsector. In 1997 and 2007 Telecom companies were part of this group but have now dropped out.

Communication Services and one is Consumer Discretionary). Unlike in the technology boom of the late 1990s, the change in leadership was not driven by high valuations but by earnings growth. Notwithstanding their increasing relevance, the five IT and related stocks trade on a combined 2019 economic P/E of $25.1 \times$, a marginal discount to US equities[3], which trade at $25.3 \times$ expected earnings.

The rise of the intangible economy

Of course, market leadership changes are not new. As economies evolve, the factors that drive their growth evolve. Western agrarian economies depended upon access to cultivable land, labour, livestock and marketplaces for trading their produce. Industrial revolutions brought fundamental changes to this operating model, introducing tools and processes to accelerate the production, processing and transportation of the goods that the economy produced. Access to the technologies and infrastructure became the key differentiators of economic performance. Railways were a transforming innovation in the 19th century. Not only did they decrease transportation costs but they also employed vast numbers of people and opened access to new markets, all of which drove economic growth.

Changes in an economy have historically resulted in adjustments to the components of equity benchmarks. There is a great deal of information on the components of the Dow Jones Industrial Average (DJIA) (Fig. 8.4). Its precursor, first published in 1884, contained nine railway stocks (out of 14 stocks in total), underscoring the importance of railways to the US economy at the time. This domination by railroads was subsequently eclipsed by the rising importance of automobiles, which also brought deep structural changes to the economy. Autos stocks made up almost a fifth of the DJIA in the 1920s. After World War II, pent-up demand and emerging prosperity led to a boom in consumer demand. The valuation of consumer stocks soared. This was repeated, mutatis mutandis, with Energy in the 1970s and IT and Internet in the 1990s. Since then, the baton has been passed to the 'new economy' companies. This may not seem evident by looking at the 30 companies that make up the DJIA, but it is clear when you look at the weight of some of the largest names in the S&P500. Modern day technology and knowhow have become the driving forces of today's economy. The companies at the vanguard of this trend are transforming the life of the average person just as fundamentally as the industrial revolution did to the

---

3. Based on CROCI's US coverage. Data as on 13 February 2019.

1896	July 1959	January 2019
American Cotton Oil	Allied Chemical	3M
American Sugar	General Electric	American Express
American Tobacco	Sears	Apple
Chicago Gas	AlCoA	Boeing
Distilling & Cattle Feeding	General Foods	Caterpillar
General Electric	Standard Oil of California	Chevron
Laclede Gas	American Can	Cisco Systems
National Lead.	General Motors	CocaCola
North American	Standard Oil of NJ (now Exxon)	DowDuPont
Tennessee Coal, Iron and Railroad	AT&T	ExxonMobil (Standard Oil of NJ)
U.S. Leather	Goodyear Tire	Goldman Sachs
United States Rubber	Swift & Co.	The Home Depot
	American Tobacco	IBM
	Int'l Harvester	Intel
	Texaco	Johnson & Johnson
	Anaconda Copper	JPMorgan Chase
	Int'l Nickel	McDonald's
	Union Carbide	Merck & Co
	Bethlehem Steel	Microsoft
	Int'l Paper	Nike
	United Aircraft	Pfizer
	Chrysler	Procter & Gamble
	Johns-Manville	Travelers
	United States Steel	UnitedHealth Group
	E.I. du Pont de Nem	United Technologies
	Owens-Illinois	Verizon
	Westinghouse Electric.	Visa
	Eastman Kodak	Walmart
	Procter & Gamble	Walgreens Boots
	Woolworth	Walt Disney

FIGURE 8.4 Dow Jones industrial average constituents. *Data from S&P Dow Jones Indices LLC and Bloomberg Finance L.P.*

agrarian economy. It's little surprise that some commentators are calling this transformation the Fourth Industrial Revolution'.[4] It is also important to realise that this revolution is not limited to the Technology sector. Retailers, Consumer Goods and even Industrial companies have significantly changed the capital structure of their businesses.

Weak revenue growth for the average listed stock

There are phenomenal changes taking place against a backdrop characterised by earnings stagnation and limited revenue growth. Median revenue growth for listed equities has been declining up till 2016 when it hit bottom at 1.1%. US tax

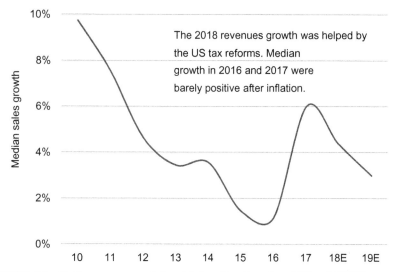

The 2018 revenues growth was helped by the US tax reforms. Median growth in 2016 and 2017 were barely positive after inflation.

FIGURE 8.5 Median revenue growth for global equities. *Data from DWS and CROCI.*

reforms briefly pushed revenues up, but now they are fading again (Fig. 8.5).

The lack of revenue growth in aggregate suggests that the world of listed equities is in full stagnation. A comparable universe of companies with full data going back to 1989[5] has gone without growth since 2007: (1) the annual pace of economic earnings growth has been 0.7%[6] since 2007 (down from 8% in the

---

4. The Fourth Industrial Revolution, Klaus Schwab, World Economic Forum 2016. The First Industrial Revolution used water and steam power to mechanize production. The Second used electric power to create mass production. The Third used electronics and information technology to automate production. Now a Fourth Industrial Revolution is building on the third.

5. This smaller subgroup consists of 300 companies with a combined market capitalisation of USD 16.9 trillion (half the market cap of our full coverage).

6. Annualised growth between 2007 and 2018

previous 8 years), (2) 2018 aggregate nominal revenues were in line with 2008 revenues and below the nominal levels seen in 2011, 2012 and 2013 and (3) cash returns have come under pressure since peaking in 2005 and 2006 as margin increases have not offset the fall in capital productivity. The current universe, including companies listed in the past decade, looks only marginally better.

Asset-light companies have delivered higher earnings growth

The weakness in growth is not uniform, however. Some sectors (IT and Health Care for example) have managed to deliver strong earnings growth, whilst others have lagged. The sectors that have managed to deliver growth can be classified as 'asset-light', whereas those that have delivered negative growth since 2007 are all 'asset-rich', requiring large fixed capital investments to generate revenues and earnings.

Fig. 8.6 shows the annualised aggregated earnings growth of various economic sectors between 2007 and 2018. The strongest growth has come from the IT sector. Health Care and legacy Consumer Discretionary[7] are next best. The newly formed Communication Services sector consists of the old Telecom Services sector and Media and Entertainment (companies previ-

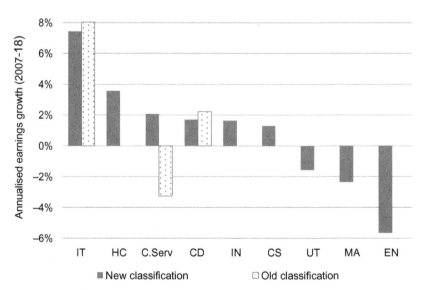

FIGURE 8.6 Annualised economic earnings growth by global sector 2007−2018. *Data from DWS and CROCI. 'Old classification' of Communication Services represents the legacy Telecommunication Services. Agglomerated data of companies in CROCI's coverage.*

---

7. The GICS classification was altered on 30 September, 2018, resulting in a new GICS sector Communication Services, which also affected the scope of Consumer Discretionary.

ously part of the IT and Consumer Discretionary sectors). The aggregate 2% annual growth in real economic earnings all comes from Media and Entertainment. The more capital-intensive Telecoms sector has lagged. The growth statistics of the other physical-asset-driven sectors (namely, Energy, Materials and Utilities) is similar. All have delivered negative real economic earnings growth. Ever since the 2009 financial crisis, policymakers have questioned why companies are not investing. Common sense suggests that companies will not invest when earnings are not growing, which explains the weakness in fixed capital expenditure observed since the 2008 financial crisis. Faced by uncertain return prospects, companies operating in capital-intensive sectors have deferred expenditure on fixed assets. The disparity in growth between the asset-light and the asset-rich sectors also points to a more fundamental change taking place within the broader economy. Asset-light companies are managing to grow despite the weak macroeconomic environment (Fig. 8.7).

2019E	CROCI	EV / NCI	Ec. PE	Ec. Earn'gs Gth. Rank
Comm. Svcs.	6.6%	1.82x	27.5x	3
Discretionary	5.1%	1.57x	31.0x	4
Staples	13.2%	3.49x	26.5x	6
Energy	3.0%	0.81x	27.0x	9
Health care	16.0%	3.48x	21.8x	2
Industrials	8.2%	1.98x	24.2x	5
IT	15.7%	3.81x	24.3x	1
Materials	5.8%	1.32x	23.0x	8
Utilities	3.1%	0.96x	31.0x	7

FIGURE 8.7   Cash returns and valuation by global sector. *Data from DWS and CROCI. Sector ranks are based on economic earnings growth between 2007 and 2018.*

Only companies with intangible assets have been able to generate earnings growth recently

The easy solution is to focus on a few sectors such as IT or Health Care. However, doing so would not fully describe the widening impact of this trend that affects most sectors. It was decided to follow a different approach and instead distinguish between companies where CROCI capitalises intangibles and companies where it does not. At an aggregate level (Fig. 8.8), it is clear that companies with intangible assets have been able to grow their earnings, unlike companies with only physical capital. Between 2007 and 2018, companies with intangible assets have had much stronger earnings growth than the remainder of our global comparable coverage. As this phenomenon could potentially be the result of a few abnormally large companies, any size bias was removed by looking at the proportion of IC-owning companies that managed to grow their earnings versus companies without IC (Fig. 8.9). It was not a surprise to discover that only companies with intangible assets were able to grow their real earnings. A final test is for sector effects: do we have similar results within the same sector? The outcome is broadly in favour of companies with IC. Again, companies with intangible assets have been able to grow their earnings at a higher rate than companies reliant only on fixed assets (Fig. 8.10).

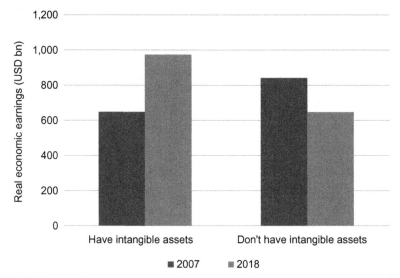

FIGURE 8.8   Earnings growth has come from companies with intellectual capital. *Data from DWS and CROCI.*

	# of companies	Median growth (annualised '2007-'18)
Companies with brands	80	3.4%
Companies with R&D	286	3.0%
Companies without IC	421	−0.6%
Total	787	1.4%

FIGURE 8.9   Median earnings growth for the entire universe. *Data from DWS and CROCI. This table excludes certain companies with negative earnings whose growth could not be calculated.*

Median 2007-18 annualised growth	Companies with intangible assets	Companies that don't have intangible assets
Communication services	13.5%	–4.9%
Consumer discretionary	2.8%	2.9%
Consumer staples	2.7%	–1.0%
Health care	4.5%	3.8%
Industrials	1.9%	1.5%
IT	4.4%	4.1%
Materials	3.8%	–3.4%

FIGURE 8.10 Median earnings growth: by sectors. *Data from DWS and CROCI. This table excludes Energy, Financials and Utilities companies as there are not enough companies for the analysis to be meaningful.*

Share price performance has followed earnings growth

As one would expect, this higher earnings growth has been rewarded by the market. Companies with intellectual capital have seen their aggregate market values double since 2007. By comparison, the market value is almost unchanged for the rest of our coverage relative to the 2007 level (Fig. 8.11).

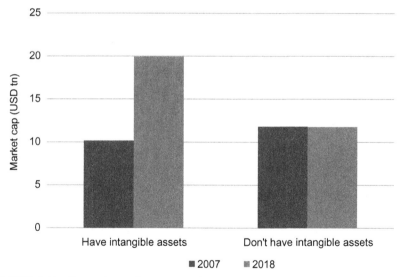

FIGURE 8.11 Share price performance has followed earnings growth. *Data from DWS and CROCI. Aggregate data of companies with comparable data going back to 2007.*

Intangible intensity not a driver of performance

Intangibles are an important driver of performance, but intangible intensity is not. One could easily imagine that the higher the spending in R&D or advertising, the better the resulting growth rate and performance. However, this is not the case. With intangibles correctly included on companies' balance sheets, it becomes much easier to compare intangible intensity across different sectors. A company's intangible intensity is defined as the proportion of that company's total assets made up by intangible assets. Health Care and IT (Fig. 8.12) have the highest median intangible intensity. But there is a broad range of intensities, even within sectors that are generally perceived as innovative. On the other hand, there are some Materials companies that are fairly innovative, such as speciality chemical companies.

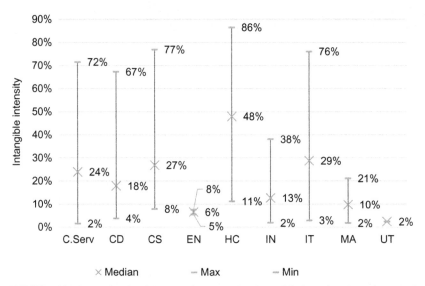

FIGURE 8.12 Innovation itself is more important that intangible intensity. *Data from DWS and CROCI. The chart shows the median intangible intensity of the global GICS economic sectors and the maximum and minimum within the sectors.*

Intangible intensity is not a driver of stock performance

A Fama-French style analysis, where stocks are ranked based on their intangible intensity and grouped into deciles, shows little difference between stocks with high and low intangible intensities within CROCI's coverage universe, as shown in Fig. 8.13. The first two deciles (comprising stocks with highest intangible intensity) may have outperformed the lowest intangible intensity deciles, but the strongest performance over this period actually comes from the fifth decile, whilst the weakest comes from the third decile (above-average intangible intensity). Although this may seem surprising, the result is consistent with other observations. In the pharmaceutical sector, for example, no evidence suggests that spending increases correspond to higher numbers of new patents. In fact, many large companies are only able to off-set declines in profitability through acquisitions. In 2010, Apple only spent 2.7% of its revenues on R&D whilst Microsoft spent over 14%. But Apple was able to generate far greater growth in profits over the following decade than Microsoft. The US manufacturing sector in the 1960s provides another striking example. The sharpest competition came from smaller companies. But if size was all that mattered, concentration in the market would have increased rather decreased.

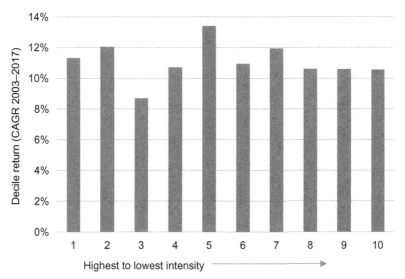

FIGURE 8.13 Performance of deciles defined by intangible intensity of their capital invested. Intangible intensity did not have an impact on performance. *Data from DWS and CROCI. Deciles are rebalanced monthly using the data that were available at the time of rebalancing. Return is calculated on a buy and hold basis and assumes no transaction costs. Return between 31 December 2003 and 29 December 2017.*

Earnings growth reflect underlying macroeconomic changes

These dynamics reflect changes taking place in the underlying economy. For instance, on the expectation of dramatic changes to the economy the Technology-Media-Telecoms frenzy led to an equities bubble in 2000. Twenty years on, many of the changes anticipated in 2000 have actually taken place. Our living and working styles have been profoundly affected. New economy companies now dominate every aspect of modern life, provid-ing the hardware for accessing and searching the internet. Consumers have one platform for obtaining news and contacting others and another platform for buying things. The position of the large IT companies must remind students of economic history of the famous monopolies enjoyed a century ago by companies such as Standard Oil. It is certainly fair to say that a few IT stocks now have economic power and wealth similar to the old Rockefeller hegemony.

The labour-light economy and the decline of middle-skilled labour

Changes in the structure of the economy are especially evident when looking at sectors such as retailing. The Centre for Retail Research in the United Kingdom shows that 148,000 jobs were lost in UK retail and hospitality over the course of 2018 while almost 20,000 shops and restaurants closed down.[8] Retailing was a stable industry for decades. Naturally there were changes in the ways the industry operated. For instance, shopping malls and large out-of-town supermarkets emerged thanks to the increasing penetration of autos and white goods during the 1950s and 1960s. 'Location, location, location' was the driver of the industry's structure. Suddenly the internet made location irrelevant, leading to fundamental changes. Access to stores is now increasingly through portals. One can shop anywhere at any time. Machine-learning software is now aware of shoppers' habits, frequently presenting buyers with options that suit their individual tastes and needs. Physical stores and the customer service traditionally provided by vendors are less important. The discounting power generated by scale and the limited requirement for traditional bricks and mortar investment have revolutionised retailing.

Technology is polarising the job market and is changing the structure of the economy

In 1931, John Maynard Keynes warned about the risks of unemployment due to technologies capable of economising the use of labour at a rate outpacing our ability to find new uses for labour (Economic possibilities for our grandchildren, 1931). One should not be overly pessimistic about the long term, but there is little doubt that technological improvements will continue to bring deep changes to the economy and society. In a paper published in 2016, Berger and Frey, from the Oxford Martin Programme on Technology and Employment, argue that technological change since the computer revolution has reduced demand for workers with middle skills and increased demand for high skills and low skills, resulting in a more polarised society. They also estimate that only 0.5% of the workforce is employed in industries that did not exist at the turn of the century. This compared with 8% of new

---

8. 150,000 high street jobs lost in 2018, *Retail Gazette*, 24th December 2018, https://www.retail-gazette.co.uk/blog/2018/12/150000-high-street-jobs-lost-2018/

jobs created by new industries in the 1980s and 4.5% of new jobs created by new industries in the 1990s. Thus they suggest that new technology is responsible for a more polarised job market that does not create many new jobs.

The nature of technological development is a key driver behind widening earnings disparities. The low growth in jobs in new technologies can also explain the anaemic rate of economic growth. Frey and Osborne[9] argue that 47% of US jobs are at risk to automation in the coming decade. This is especially the case in transportation and logistics, together with the bulk of office and administrative support workers and labour in production occupations (Fig. 8.14).

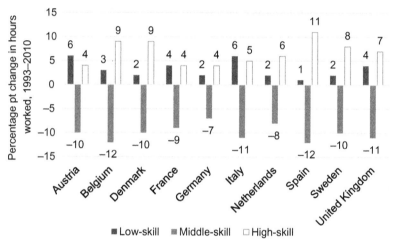

FIGURE 8.14 Labour market polarisation. *Data from Goos, M., Manning, A., Salomons, A., 2014. Explaining job polarization: routine-biased technological change and offshoring. Am. Econ. Rev. 104 (8), 2509−2526. Copyright American Economic Association; reproduced with permission of the American Economic Review.*

The increasing importance of brands within the economy

If the importance of R&D and new technology is becoming increasingly evident, brands are also playing critical roles. The concept behind brands is not new, of course. They have historically been associated with companies popularising an image of a physical product. When a consumer sees the actual product in a supermarket or on the high street, she prefers it to a generic product. In a world that separates physical capital and the act of distributing a product, brands can clinch a sale.

---

9. Frey & Osborne, The Future of Employment: How Susceptible are Jobs to Computerisation, Oxford Martin School, 2013

CROCI intellectual capital

The valuation conundrum

It is not straightforward to identify with certainty the reasons behind luke-warm earnings growth. One line of thinking is that weak earnings growth since the 2008 financial crisis was a function of the inability of new technologies to generate new jobs while at the same time disrupting the middle-skilled job market. Labour market polarisation, the rise of the gig economy and growing disparity in income and wealth distribution are the results of this change. In this evolutionary context, it makes sense for investors to protect themselves by not investing in companies dependent exclusively on fixed assets. It seems reasonable to expect companies without any IC to trade at a discount to the broader market, given the structural challenges that they face. In fact, though, they sell at a premium (Fig. 8.15) while embodying lower growth and higher leverage risk.

2018	With IC	Without IC (ex Fin.)	Financials
Valuation			
Accounting P/E	18.8x	14.7x	9.7x
Economic P/E	23.7x	26.6x	16.2x
EV/NCI (Adj. CROCI P/B)	2.88x	1.30x	1.31x
Annualised 5Y growth			
Sales growth	2.7%	−1.3%	−
Real economic earnings	5.7%	−2.3%	6.9%
Profitability and cash flow			
CROCI (RoC for financials)	12.1%	4.9%	11.2%
FCF / sales (post-tax)	9.7%	5.1%	−
Leverage			
Net financial liabs / M. Cap	18.3%	50.7%	−

FIGURE 8.15 Operational and valuation characteristics of companies with and without intellectual capital. *Data from DWS and CROCI.*

Companies without IC generate a cash return of 4.9% below cost of capital. Despite this, the group trades on an EV/NCI (economic price-to-book) of 1.30 ×. Meanwhile, the IC group's EV/NCI is 2.88 ×, reflecting its much higher cash return of 12.1%. Figs 8.16 and 8.17 further indicate the significant differential of real economic earnings between companies with and without intellectual capital. Although growth in both was relatively similar between 1989 and 2007, this trend has dramatically diverged over the past 10 years.

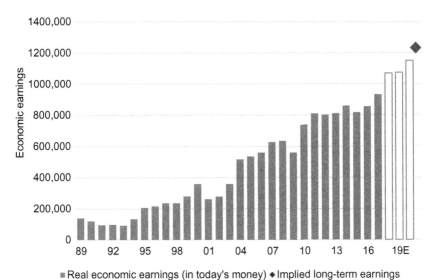

■ Real economic earnings (in today's money) ◆ Implied long-term earnings

FIGURE 8.16 Economic earnings of companies with intellectual capital. *Data from DWS and CROCI.*

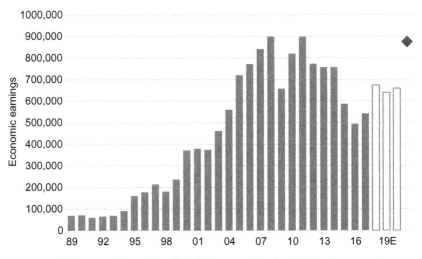

■ Real economic earnings (in today's money) ◆ Implied long-term earnings

FIGURE 8.17 Economic earnings of companies without intellectual capital. *Data from DWS and CROCI.*

Investment strategy for the knowledge driven economy

So, how should investors position themselves to benefit from this structural shift? Thematic investing has been on the rise over the past few years, but investors should shy away from ultraspecialised approaches. The rise and fall of cryptocurrency in 2018 and the 2001 dot-com bubble provide poignant reminders of the risks that lurk. In the latter example, investors correctly judged the Internet to be a major driver of future commerce. But many of the companies designed to take advantage of that future didn't survive the crash that followed. Such trend-following commonly drives up valuations, encouraging the spread of companies with dubious business models.

A Real Investor requires something broader, something that captures the structural rise of the theme across multiple industries and regions/markets. In particular, such an investment strategy ought to:

1. Take into consideration all listed firms that have intangible assets, regardless of sector or region, including emerging markets.
2. Remove unnecessary risks, in particular avoiding:
    a. Poor profitability. Investments in intangibles that do not enhance profitability are of little use to investors. Companies at the bottom-end of the profitability scale vs. their peers clearly lack this advantage. In any case, it is hard to argue that companies with continued weak profitability will be able to grow their earnings or even survive in the long term.
    b. High financial leverage. This is a risk that overlaps with the one above. High debt levels introduce additional risks. At companies that don't have high returns, high debt levels commonly indicate an inability to generate cash organically, preventing sustainable earnings growth.
    c. Poor ESG rating. Growing with poor governance or at the expense of others is not sustainable in the long term. Investors are unwilling to risk such exposure in a world characterised by ever increasing scrutiny.
3. Focus on companies that are able to leverage their intellectual capital to drive profitability and earnings growth.
4. Avoid overpaying. A company's weight in the portfolio should mirror its real level of earnings rather than its market cap, which risks embedding excess expectations.
5. Reassess changes in the market's economic structure on a regular basis. The process is reviewed every 3 months to ensure to capture new entrants and changes taking place in the underlying economics of the businesses.

Performance, sector and regional characteristics

A simulation of this approach (Fig. 8.18) over the 2004–18 period[10] produced the following results:

1. This investment strategy delivered a 9.3% annual return up to the end of 2018, outperforming the MSCI All Countries by 270 bps. The volatility of this strategy was 12.9%, a full 160 bps below the benchmark.
2. The strategy outperformed the benchmark in all but 4 years over this period. In 2 of those 4 years – 2005 and 2006 – the underperformance was caused by substantial outperformance in the Financials and Real Estate sectors. The only other year showing a material underperformance was 2016, when high capital-intensity sectors with high operational leverage outperformed on expectations of Trumponomics.
3. A multifactor attribution of the record shows that outperformance comes from (1) specific factors (stock selection), (2) sector and (3) country bets. Style exposure ('risk indices') is generally neutral.
4. The strategy ended up with exposure to just 7 of the 10 economic sectors. IT, Health Care and Consumer Staples had the largest weights and the strategy also received meaningful exposure to the Consumer Discretionary, Industrials and Materials sectors.
5. Historically the strategy overweighted different sectors and regions depending on their abilities to leverage intellectual capital to drive earnings growth. The strategy seeks exposure to this ability regardless of the region or sector classification of individual companies.

	CROCI IC	MSCI World	MSCI ACWI
Comp. annual growth	9.3%	6.6%	6.6%
Annualised monthly vol	12.9%	14.5%	14.9%
Sharpe ratio (1.41%)	0.61	0.36	0.34
% of months with gains	64.0%	62.9%	61.8%
Tracking error		4.1%	4.5%
Information ratio		0.66	0.61
Worst drawdown	−43.1%	−53.7%	−54.6%
Time to recov. (month)	33	69	69

FIGURE 8.18 Simulated performance analysis of CROCI IC vs MSCI World and MSCE ACWI. *Data from DWS and CROCI. The chart shows simulated Strategy performance between 27 February 2004 and 31 December 2018. The performance is calculated by retroactive application of the strategy model.*

10. The CROCI as-seen company database begins in early 2004. Using this allows simulations to avoid any survivorship bias, amongst other things.

Operational characteristics and an evolutionary conclusion

The operational characteristics of the CROCI intellectual capital investment strategy (Fig. 8.19) include:

1. **High Cash Returns.** A weighted average cash return of 23% (5 pp ahead of the market-cap-weighted selection pool). This cash return is driven by higher margins whilst asset productivity (sales/gross capital invested) is slightly below the selection pool. Higher cash returns are a sign of a competitive advantage.
2. **Attractive valuations:** both on economic *P/E* and FCF yield.
3. **Revenue growth at 8%.**
4. **Financial leverage of only 6.7%.** The weighted average for the selection pool is 31.8%.

FY1 data on 31 December 2018	CROCI IC	Investable universe
Profitability		
CROCI	23.0%	18.0%
EBITDA margin	30.5%	27.1%
Sales/gross capital invested	0.86x	0.90x
Sales growth	8.0%	8.8%
Cash generation		
FCF/sales	17.3%	13.6%
FCF after dividends/sales	12.3%	8.1%
Valuation and Leverage		
EV/NCI (Economic P/B)	5.62x	5.02x
Economic P/E	18.4x	24.9x
Accounting P/E	14.2x	15.1x
FCF yield	5.7%	4.6%
Dividend yield	2.2%	2.7%
Net fin. liabilities/Mkt Cap	6.7%	31.8%

FIGURE 8.19 Operational characteristics of CROCI IC versus the CROCI investable universe. *Data from DWS and CROCI.*

Conclusion

Some investors might consider systematic approach to intellectual capital to be controversial. Several issues could be raised, such as the potentially short-term nature of themes in the market. But that is why intellectual capital does not focus on narrow themes like single sectors (Health Care, say) or specific fads (such as Social Media). Instead, this chapter sheds light on how evolutionary economies and equity markets tend to be, something that is often overlooked. Most companies cannot be considered perpetuities, true even at the most elite level.

Beyond CROCI intellectual capital, understanding how an economy and a benchmark evolves over time can be an important source of performance for investors. At the same time, it is essential for the Real Investors that valuation remains in focus so as to avoid any speculative drive.

Appendix

Why investors cannot ignore intangible assets[11]

There are two types of intangible assets that generate cash flow within companies but are routinely missing from balance sheets – R&D and brands. Accounting standards conventionally treat the expenditure that creates such assets (R&D and advertising cost) as operating costs, but this should not be the case. These expenditures tend to be important drivers of companies' earnings – patents and knowhow in the Health Care sector, for example – and need to be capitalised on balance sheets, just like expenditures on physical fixed assets. This issue may not be relevant to an accountant, but it is of fundamental importance to investors.

What about goodwill paid by an acquirer during an acquisition – how does CROCI treat that? This goodwill can generally be split into two components. One part is the crystallisation of the cash-generative assets of the type mentioned above: brands or R&D that are not on the accounting balance sheet. The other element tends not to generate cash flow, though, and can be thought of as the genuine premium paid over asset values. This is not an operating asset, so it is excluded from the analysis.

There is wide evidence for the relevance of intangible capital

Estimating the economic life of intangibles requires in-depth fundamental analysis and time. References emerge when we diligently scour company accounts and other primary sources. The FDA database has, for example, extensive information related to R&D in the Health Care sector. IT

---

11. Intangibles is a fundamental adjustment made to the accounts and has already been discussed in chapter two. Here I analyse the issue in further details.

companies occasionally provide important anecdotes, such as how long it has taken to develop new software, and we also know how often those assets are replaced. For companies where loyalty is generated by advertising (luxury goods or noncyclical consumer goods), the economic life is based on estimations of what happens to sales when marketing campaigns conclude.

This analysis can be difficult, but it is better to be approximately correct than precisely mistaken. Even so, the CROCI approach remains conservative. For instance, it does not capitalise brands in IT and pharmaceutical companies as R&D is the source of their competitive advantage. Sony, Nokia, Motorola and AOL were all household names until their product leadership faded. Their brand names soon followed.

Sceptics might well argue that this approach is subjective but the same is true for other fixed assets. Estimation of the useful life of intangible assets is not very different from that of fixed assets. The capitalisation of fixed assets in the cement and steel industry in China assumes that the current rate of investment in infrastructure, which some deem unsustainable, will be maintained over the next two decades. When the investment rate eventually comes down, assets employed in such industries will need to be written off. This is just another way of saying that the economic lives of those assets are actually shorter than the periods over which these companies are depreciating their assets. Assuming that asset lives are longer naturally results in lower depreciation charges and therefore provides an artificial boost in earnings.

The US GDP Statistics Office has also been capitalising research and development expenditure since 2015. R&D investments are reported in 'intellectual property products'. Within the CROCI Investment and Valuation Group, we have recognised the need to capitalise R&D costs since 1996.

CROCI treats intellectual capital as a genuine asset

Companies with intellectual capital are ubiquitous

As expected, intangible assets are clearly more important in certain sectors than in others (Figs 8.20 and 8.21). For example, four-fifths of Health Care companies have intellectual capital. Even so, sectors that are not as closely associated with intellectual capital, such as Industrials and Consumer Discretionary, possess intellectual capital assets. Nearly two-fifths of CROCI's coverage in both these sectors have intellectual capital. Even Materials and Energy sectors have such assets, albeit more localised in narrow subsectors such as Speciality Chemicals and Drillers (Fig. 8.22).

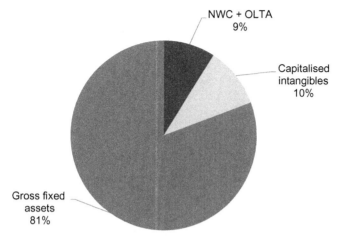

FIGURE 8.20 Asset composition of the investable universe. *Data from DWS and CROCI.*

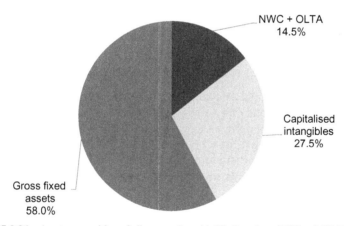

FIGURE 8.21 Asset composition of all companies with IC. *Data from DWS and CROCI.*

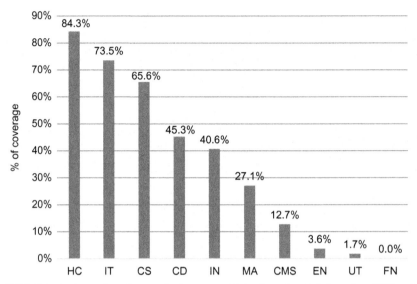

FIGURE 8.22 Proportion of companies by sector with intellectual capital. *Data from DWS and CROCI.*

Capitalising intangibles can substantially alter profitability

Adding intellectual capital to companies' balance sheets can have a significant impact on profitability as well as valuation ratios.

The impact is not uniform though. The degree to which profitability falls depends upon the relative mix of reported and hidden assets on balance sheets as well as the expenditure on those assets and the period over which economic benefits from those expenditures are likely to flow to the company.

As Fig. 8.23 shows, the useful lives of these assets vary depending upon the type of the asset, the sector in which the company operates and unique characteristics of those assets. For example, intangible expenditure forms a large part of a pharmaceutical company's capital expenditure and the resulting assets have a long life. The result is that the total capital employed in pharmaceutical companies is over $3 \times$ times their reported assets. *Caeteris paribus*, the same level of profits over a much larger asset base will bring down the expected rate of return on equities as well as the price-to-book ratio. The impact such capitalisation can have on reported assets and profitability is significant.

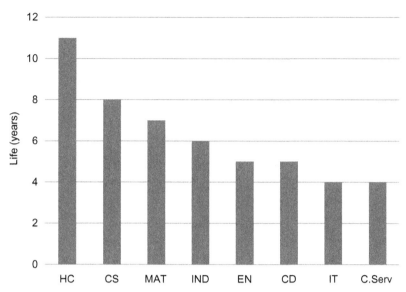

FIGURE 8.23   Estimated life of capitalised intangibles. *Data from DWS and CROCI.*

The CROCI companies come from the three sectors with the highest concentrations of intangible assets. Each company spends between 13% and 17% of its sales on intangibles. But because of the differences in the useful lives of the resulting assets, their capitalised values vary (Fig. 8.24).

2017 data (mn)	Microsoft (USD)	Sanofi (EUR)	Coca-Cola (USD)
Intangible type	Software R&D	Pharma R&D	Brands
Average life of intangibles	4y	12y	15y
% of sales capitalized	13%	15%	17%
Assets			
Shareholder equity ex GW	41,286	5,330	363
CROCI net cap. intangibles	24,494	29,785	38,431
CROCI net cap. invested ex GW	87,347	50,224	50,625
Intangible intensity	28%	59%	76%
Profitability (ex GW)			
ROE	73.9%	100.8%	896.4%
CROCI	27.5%	11.7%	11.8%
EV/NCI	7.71x	2.13x	3.69x
P/B (ex goodwill)	16.2x	19.4x	528.3x

FIGURE 8.24   Impact of capitalisation on reported assets and profitability. *Data from DWS and CROCI.*

These intangibles make up 28% of CROCI's estimate of Microsoft's net capital invested but 76% of Coca Cola's.

The capitalised intangibles have a substantial impact on the profitability of these companies. All three companies look profitable according to conventional measures but less so once all their assets are taken into account. In the case of Coca Cola, the return on equity of 896% translates into a CROCI of just 11.8%.

Capitalising intangibles and the economics of sectors

The economics of the various sectors post the capitalisation of intangibles are illustrated in Fig. 8.25 and shows:

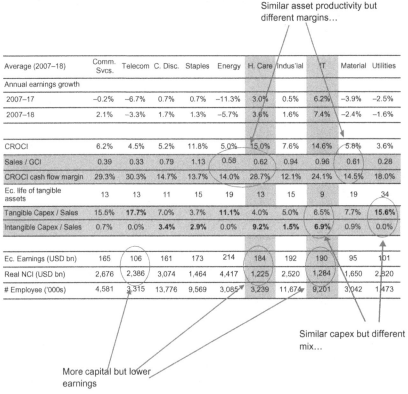

Average (2007–18)	Comm. Svcs.	Telecom	C. Disc.	Staples	Energy	H. Care	Indus'ial	IT	Material	Utilities
Annual earnings growth										
2007–17	−0.2%	−6.7%	0.7%	0.7%	−11.3%	3.0%	0.5%	6.2%	−3.9%	−2.5%
2007–18	2.1%	−3.3%	1.7%	1.3%	−5.7%	3.6%	1.6%	7.4%	−2.4%	−1.6%
CROCI	6.2%	4.5%	5.2%	11.8%	5.0%	15.0%	7.6%	14.6%	5.8%	3.6%
Sales / GCI	0.39	0.33	0.79	1.13	0.58	0.62	0.94	0.96	0.61	0.28
CROCI cash flow margin	29.3%	30.3%	14.7%	13.7%	14.0%	28.7%	12.1%	24.1%	14.5%	18.0%
Ec. life of tangible assets	13	13	11	15	19	13	15	9	19	34
Tangible Capex / Sales	15.5%	17.7%	7.0%	3.7%	11.1%	4.0%	5.0%	6.5%	7.7%	15.6%
Intangible Capex / Sales	0.7%	0.0%	3.4%	2.9%	0.0%	9.2%	1.5%	6.9%	0.9%	0.0%
Ec. Earnings (USD bn)	165	106	161	173	214	184	192	190	95	101
Real NCI (USD bn)	2,676	2,386	3,074	1,464	4,417	1,225	2,520	1,284	1,650	2,820
# Employee ('000s)	4,581	3,315	13,776	9,569	3,085	3,239	11,674	9,201	3,042	1,473

Similar asset productivity but different margins…

Similar capex but different mix…

More capital but lower earnings

FIGURE 8.25 Operational characteristics: global coverage by sectors. *Data from DWS and CROCI.*

1. The IT sector invests as much (as a percentage of revenues) as the Utilities sector (13.4% vs 15.6%) and more than Energy (13.4% vs 11.1%), but its split is very different, with 6.5% in tangible capex and 6.9% in R&D. Investments made in Utilities and Energy only take the form of tangible capital.
2. Capital invested in IT and Health Care is a fraction of the capital employed in Utilities, Telecoms and Energy, but the former generate a much higher level of economic earnings.
3. Health Care, Materials and Energy have similar levels of capital intensity (Fig. 8.26). They generate the same sales output per unit of gross inflation-adjusted capital, but Health Care has a much higher margin, a sign of a strong competitive advantage. IT and Industrials also have the same capital productivity but very different margins.
4. Telecoms have the highest margins and the lowest capital productivity, which is why the sector only manages to deliver a 4.5% CROCI. Their capital productivity is similar to that of the Utilities sector, but companies in the latter have even lower margins.
5. Let's not forget that margin ought to be a function of capital intensity. The higher the required capital, the higher the margins ought to be. Margins in isolation can only tell part of the story.

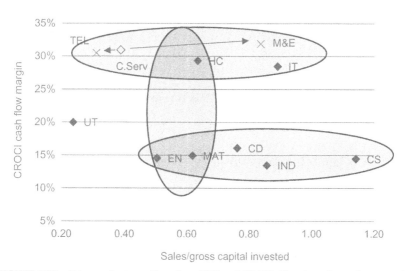

FIGURE 8.26 Drivers of returns. *Data from DWS and CROCI. The chart shows the two main drivers of cash returns, namely, cash flow margins and capital intensity (sales/gross capital invested) of nonfinancial sectors.*

Intangibles in financials

In 2009 Paul Volcker gave an interesting talk at the Wall Street Journal Future of Finance Initiative when he said that 'the most important financial innovation I have seen in the past 20 years is the automatic teller machine'. I believe there is no meaningful intangible asset at most large banks. This is also the case for many Food Retailers, Utilities, Energy and Telecom stocks. Some may argue their brand names are assets, but for us those brand names are of little value as those do not provide a competitive advantage. Physical location is a bigger source of competitive advantage in these sectors. This is clear from the analysis of the profitability of companies that tend to be at or below the cost of capital.

Section 3

Through the looking glass

Over the past few years, I have come across a number of simple issues where our analysis said something different from the mainstream way of thinking. I found that nothing was quite what it seemed, whether it was about (1) markets being cheap in the 1970s, (2) inflation being good for equities, (3) Emerging Markets being better investments than Developed Markets, (4) risk premia in sectors or regions or (5) bubbles. In my journey towards a better understanding of valuation, capital and return, I have stepped through the looking glass and there is no easy way back. The focus, in this section, is on two issues: how inflation distorts the long-term valuation of equities and equity bubbles.

Introduction

The democratisation of investments in equities took place in the second half of the 20th century. From the Anglo-Saxon world, it spread to continental Europe. For large countries such as China and India, this process is just beginning. In practice, our understanding of equities is still in the making. The excessive focus on price dynamics, the superficial attitude of policy-makers towards equities, the use of accounting data for investment purposes, and the very high number of books written by practitioners are signs of a relatively young discipline. Within this context, it was no surprise to see the 2013 Nobel Prize was awarded to three economists, Lars Peter Hansen, Eugene Fama and Robert Shiller, two of whom (Fama and Shiller) take very different views about the world of investment.[1] My personal interpretation of the award is 'there is a fundamental lack of understanding of markets and market dynamics. Even if you do not agree on how markets work and we do

---

1. The efficient-market hypothesis was developed by Eugene Fama, building on work by Louis Bachelier and others. Fama argues that markets are always efficient. Shiller is associated with Fama for his work on the equity valuation over the very long term and the role that human psychology plays. The obvious question is how can psychology have a role in a fully efficient market?

not know who is right, through your debate we have a better understanding of equities'.

I am confident that investors will develop a better understanding of equities and investments. The price of equities is the price of capital and as such provides a fundamental barometer of investor sentiment. At a conference in early 2019 I was lucky enough to be able to ask a question of a Fed Governor. 'The price of assets (equities) has been coming down since the summer. Bottom-up data on the top 900 companies around the world suggest capital investments will be down in 2019. Revenue growth is running in the low single digits for the same group. In their fourth quarter reporting companies have been suggesting that the consumer is feeling the pinch. However, you are set on rising rates. Why do central banks never look at indicators coming from equities?' The answer was that their leading indicators suggested all was well.

The simple reality is that central banks still have little interest in equity markets and market driven indicators. Equities are still considered a market for speculators. This should not be the case, and I am confident that perception will change during the next twenty years. The world of investment is evolving, and consumers are increasingly being forced to manage their retirement savings. Consumers need conditions for making appropriate investment decisions, and those conditions require more and better fundamental research.

Equities are capital. Providing capital and expecting a return are at the core of capitalist economies. Capital and capital dynamics are at the roots of decision making for central banks, governments, companies and individuals. If capital is at the centre of our economies, then understanding equities is an essential requirement for successful living in a capitalist society.

And valuation is of primary importance too. If the price of an asset is below its replacement value, James Tobin, another Nobel laureate, would argue that rational companies should buy back their capital rather than to invest. This is particularly important when looking at the European banking sector, which is trading on an adjusted price-to-book ratio of $0.9 \times$. Central banks keep on lowering rates with the hope of increasing demand for investments and deterring stagnation. However, low rates make banks' operations uneconomical, so if banks keep on deleveraging their balance sheets is it not clear that the policy is failing? Conversely, when the price-to-book of most of the market is at a multiyear high, then speculation abounds as companies build new assets. If the price of those asset is a multiple of what they spend, this behaviour results in assets being built for speculative purposes rather than fulfilling fundamental demand.

Throughout this book, I have offered the insights of a practitioner trained by academics. Having discussed such issues with many colleagues, clients, and friends, I believe some issues warrant further research. In this section, I share my findings on two issues: how inflation in the 1970s and 1980s distorted the long-term valuation of equities, and how to identify bubbles in equities and why it is important to monitor them. Both are subjects close to the hearts of Robert Shiller and Eugene Fama.

Chapter 9, Equities, inflation and valuation, focuses on inflation, valuation and the price of equities. The common perception is that markets were cheap in the 1970s and are now expensive, but this is not in fact the case. By now, the reader ought to be familiar with the distortion to valuations created by inflation. The best way to describe the 1970s is that they looked cheap but they were not cheap. I use a model that answers a simple question: *if earnings and revenues grow in line with inflation during a period of rising inflation, would you expect the price of equities to grow in a similar manner? And what would happen during a period of falling inflation?* Such a model should be used by anyone doing longitudinal analysis to compare valuations across regions and countries.

Chapter 10 is about Bubbles in equities. Fama argues that bubbles do not exist. His argument is that excessive valuation means that investors just receive a low return on equities. Still, when the price of an asset goes beyond what is fundamentally justified by its return, then there is an intrinsic interest for management to build assets for speculative purposes. This creates the boom and bust dynamic of investments and speculation, something that central banks, policymakers and investors should be aware of. I provide a framework for measuring bubbles in equities.

Chapter 11, Odysseus on valuing and investing in equities, concludes the book. As I was preparing my viva voce to defend my PhD thesis, I had to find a way to summarise the thesis in a sentence. I cannot recall if I ever managed it. Within this short chapter, I summarise in a few pages what I believe are fundamental points to be considered when valuing and investing in equities.

Chapter 9

Equities, inflation and valuation

Chapter Outline

If earnings and revenues grow in line with inflation during a period of rising inflation, would you expect the price of equities to grow in a similar manner? And what would happen during a period of falling inflation?

This chapter is quite technical in nature but it is of fundamental importance to anyone that wishes to develop a proper understanding of how inflation affects the price of equities.* The analysis demonstrates that the P/E ratio as measured by accounting data ought to fall in periods of rising inflation and rise in periods of falling inflation. The ratio confounds this intuition not because investors are fooled by inflation and are discounting earnings with a nominal rate, but because they are using reported earnings, a poor proxy for the cash earnings generated by the business. In practice, any long-term analysis looking at the valuation of

---

* Much of the material used refers to a paper 'The danger to equities from inflation', published in April 2011. Deutsche Bank, DWS. All rights reserved. Any unauthorised use is prohibited.

Valuing and Investing in Equities. DOI: https://doi.org/10.1016/B978-0-12-813848-9.00009-1

equities needs to be adjusted during periods of high inflation or else it may deliver erroneous results.

How inflation affects valuation - a model based approach

The valuation of equities over the long term is a matter of much importance for equity investors as well as for pension funds, insurance companies and asset allocators, and it also ought to define the behaviour of central bankers. However, little research has been carried out on understanding how inflation affects valuation and specifically if markets are 'cheap' when inflation is high, or not.

The work of Robert Shiller on asset prices is an important reference point for investors and researchers, particularly his longitudinal analysis of the S&P's valuation. His approach is based on the Cyclically Adjusted Price-to-Earnings ratio, which combines the current price of an asset and its long-term (10-year) average earnings. The 10-year moving average smooths the cyclicality of earnings, providing a better valuation indicator. His work going back to the late 19th century provides many insights about the very long-term valuation of equities.

Given how important CROCI adjustments are to valuation, it ought to be interesting to see what CROCI has to say on the matter. Although for most companies CROCI data goes back 30 years, for a select group of 21 companies it starts in 1981. What we found contrasted with typical expectations that markets were 'cheap' in the 1980s, in fact most companies were rather expensive. We can confirm this with the notes to the company accounts made by the companies themselves to adjust for the inflation distortion (see Appendix). This prompted my interest on three issues: (1) were markets cheap in the 1970s? (2) how does inflation affect the valuation dynamics? (3) what is the long-term valuation of equities?

Constrained by our database, I instead developed a model for a hypothetical US company that starts operating in 1950 and between 1960 and 2010 grows stated earnings, capex and revenues in line with inflation while keeping everything else constant (i.e. there is no real growth). The company:

1. has a constant capex to sales ratio of 9% and the capex has an economic life of 16 years (similar to the US market in the early 1980s),
2. has grown revenues and capex in line with US inflation since 1950,
3. has a constant net profit margin of 7%,
4. does not grow in real terms,
5. pays no taxes,
6. invests its equity only in tangible fixed assets,
7. distributes all the cash available at year end (cash earnings) to investors, and
8. assumes investors put a price of $15.0 \times$ on the cash they get; that is, investors assume that the cash they get in a year is what they will get into perpetuity and demand a constant real rate of return of 6.67%.

	1960	1965	1970	1975	1981	1991	2001	2010
CPI	1.5%	1.6%	5.9%	9.1%	10.4%	4.2%	2.8%	1.6%
Cum. inflation	100	106.6	131.3	181.9	307.4	460.3	598.4	737.1
Cum. stated earnings	100	106.6	131.3	181.9	307.4	460.3	598.4	737.1
Cum. cash earnings (CE)	100	109.4	115.8	127.4	163.9	347.7	540	698.2
Cum. acc. book	100	107.9	120.8	149.4	227.9	411.2	573.6	721.5
Cum. real book	100	106.6	131.3	181.9	307.4	460.3	598.4	737.1
Capex to sales	9%	9%	9%	9%	9%	9%	9%	9%
Depreciation to sales	7.90%	8.10%	7.20%	6.20%	5.20%	6.50%	7.40%	7.60%
Profit to sales	7%	7%	7%	7%	7%	7%	7%	7%
Cash earn. (CE) to sales	5.90%	6.10%	5.20%	4.20%	3.20%	4.50%	5.40%	5.60%
ROE	11.20%	11.10%	12.20%	13.60%	15.10%	12.50%	11.70%	11.40%
Infl adj ROE	8.20%	8.50%	7.30%	5.80%	4.40%	6.20%	7.40%	7.80%

FIGURE 9.1   Selected P&L, cash flow and balance sheet data for a hypothetical US company. Note the divergence between 'stated' and 'cash' earnings, between 'profit to sales' and 'CE to sales', and between 'ROE' and 'Infl. adj ROE'. *From the author.*

The hypothetical P&L, cash flow and balance sheet are presented in Fig. 9.1. It is clear how inflation can fool investors into believing that markets are cheap when inflation is high.[†] The results of the modelling exercise indicate that:

- In period of rising inflation (1965−1981), cash earnings grows at a lower pace than stated earnings, revenues and inflation.
- The accounting book lags inflation, which results in a higher stated ROE whilst in real terms the ROE drops between 1965 and 1981 as the level of cash earnings is lower and the capital is higher.
- By 1981 cash earnings is only 64% above the 1960 level, while the cost of living is up 300%.

Cash earnings (CE) growth lags stated earnings and revenue growth because of the time-lag between buying an asset and using the asset. The consumption of the asset is done over time, and the appropriate charge is registered in the P&L. However, in a period of high inflation, the company records a charge for an asset that was bought many years back (eight in this case). This adjustment is explained in detail in Chapter 2, Valuing non

---

†. The nature of the distortions have exposed in details in chapter three on the inflation adjustment.

financial companies. The distortion, at a practical level, is created by the stated charge underrepresenting the real charge the company is incurring in delivering its revenues. The company will need to replace the asset, and it will naturally incur a higher expenditure. This results in an overstatement of the true level of profitability. In the model, where the average age of the assets invested in the business is 8 years, the company in 1981 depreciates assets in 1973 nominal currency. That is why depreciation-to-sales rate decreases from 8.1% in 1965 to 5.2% in 1981. However, the real cash spent to replace the depreciation charge is still 9% of sales. As investors focus on cash earnings rather than stated earnings, markets appear attractively valued on accounting *P/E* even though they are not.

If investors focus on cash earnings rather than reported earnings, one should expect the *P/E* ratio to come down during periods of rising inflation and increasing in periods of falling inflation, which is effectively what happened (Fig. 9.2).

If I divide the 50 years after 1960 into two periods (Fig. 9.2), it is possible to observe that from 1960 to 1980, inflation went from low single digits to 15% and the *P/E* ratio of US companies declined from 20 × to below 10 ×, but in the second period (1980−2010), inflation decreased from 15% to low single digits and the *P/E* ratio went from high single digits to 20 ×. **Rising inflation is negative for the price of equities, and the opposite is true when inflation falls.** Modigliani and Cohn (1979) argue that equities become cheap in periods of high inflation as investors discount real cash flows at nominal rates, suggesting that the stock market suffers from money illusion. However, the model suggests this is not the case.

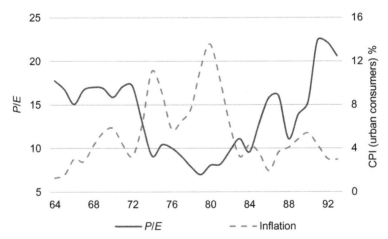

FIGURE 9.2   *P/E* ratio of the S&P 500 and inflation rate 1964−1994. The *P/E* ratio went down as inflation rose and it went up as inflation declined. *Data from Bureau of Labor Statistics, S&P, and Bloomberg. Data as available on 20 September 2019.*

Companies with different profitability and capital intensity will be affected in a different way by inflation

In assessing how inflation affects different companies, I propose two variations to the original hypothetical company, which I will call company A. In the first case, the capex-to-sales ratio (capital intensity) is higher, but everything else remains the same; that is, revenues and profits grow in line with inflation. The capex-to-sales ratio for this stock (company B) throughout the period is 15%, and investors can think of a Utility stock as its proxy. In the second case, the capex to sales ratio goes back to 9% but the net profit margin is higher, 13% versus 7% for the core case (company A). This is a company with a strong franchise, something like Healthcare stock, which I will call company C. For the three companies, the other assumptions are the same (Fig. 9.3).

The three companies are all growing revenues and earnings in line with inflation; however, it is striking to see how cash earnings has a different dynamic in each case. In periods of rising inflation, companies with the highest level of profitability actually see their level of cash earnings grow at the fastest pace. High capital intensity companies grow their cash earnings the least. By 1981, company B is producing only 36% of the cash earnings it produced in 1960 versus more than twice that for company C, even though they all grow stated earnings in line with inflation throughout the period. **With high inflation, stocks with the highest profitability should have the highest P/E ratio, whereas stocks with high capital intensity should have the lowest.**

Earnings growth in line with inflation, when inflation is rising, actually translates into falling EBITDA margins

EBITDA margin and reported earnings need to increase to offset rising inflation. The reader may have noted that our hypothetical model implicitly assumes falling EBITDA margins as inflation rises. If the ratio of depreciation-to-sales comes down and the net profit margin stays unchanged at 7%, the EBITDA margin needs to fall in line with the depreciation-to sales ratio. This is what the core model quietly implies: a decrease in

	1960	1965	1970	1975	1981	1991	2001	2010
CPI	1.5%	1.6%	5.9%	9.1%	10.4%	4.2%	2.8%	1.6%
Cumulative inflation rate	100	106.6	131.3	181.9	307.4	460.3	598.4	737.1
A,B,C cum stated earnings	100	106.6	131.3	181.9	307.4	460.3	598.4	737.1
Comp. A Cum cash earn.	100	109.4	115.8	127.4	163.9	347.7	540	698.2
Comp. B Cum cash earn.	100	111.9	101.9	87.1	35.7	247	487.7	663.3
Comp. C Cum cash earn.	100	108	123.6	145.8	236.1	404.3	569.4	717.8

FIGURE 9.3   With rising inflation, different firms may display similar growth rates for 'stated' earnings, but this is not the case for 'cash' earnings. *From the author.*

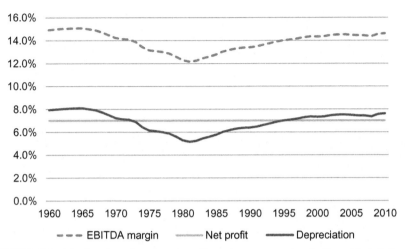

FIGURE 9.4   Margins dynamics when 'stated' earnings are growing in line with inflation. *From the author.*

EBITDA margin of 290bps between 1965 and 1981. Holding EBITDA margins constant would see stated earnings growth outpacing inflation as the depreciation-to-sales ratio falls, and in our core model cash earnings is growing in line with inflation (Fig. 9.4).

Unfortunately holding EBITDA margins constant still leads to a real loss for equity investors when inflation is rising. Even if the rate of growth in net profit is higher than inflation itself, cash earnings grows below the inflation rate as taxation increases in real terms as inflation rises, as does the replacement cost of inventories (Fig. 9.5).

The inflation cost of tax

In our core case I assume no taxation. **If the hypothetical company were taxed at a constant tax rate of 35% on pretax profits, the real rate of taxation would increase as inflation goes up.** Stated pretax profits would go up because depreciation comes down as a percentage of sales in a rising inflation environment. And this higher pretax margin attracts higher real taxation. (Whether tax is calculated from depreciation or, more usually, on accelerated capital allowances, both are subject to the historical cost of the assets rather than the replacement cost—the effect is lessened in the United States and elsewhere by capital allowances. It is also worth noting that capital losses are carried forward at nominal values and that, depending on local tax regimes, corporation taxes may include the inflation element of the gain.) Hence, assuming constant EBITDA margins, the company ends up paying a higher real tax rate. So the combination of a constant EBITDA margin and faster stated earnings growth than inflation is still not enough to protect

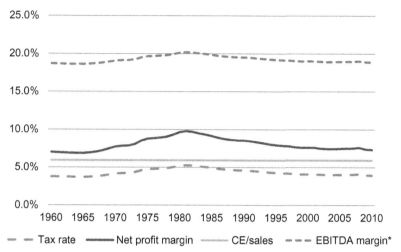

FIGURE 9.5   Margins dynamics when 'cash' earnings are growing in line with inflation. *From the author.*

investors against rising inflation. Again, the cash effect should be taken into account and modelling the future tax stream becomes imperative.

The inflation cost of inventories to investors

A constant EBITDA margin tends to overstate the real gross margin. In our hypothetical model there are no inventories, but most companies hold inventories, which have dynamics similar to tangible fixed assets. They need to be replaced, generally at a higher cost when inflation is rising. If a company sells goods that have been warehoused for a year in a country where inflation is running at 50% then, by the time the goods are sold, the company will need to spend 50% more to replace them. If the company sells the goods at a price 50% higher than they were bought for, the company will book a gross profit. In reality the company has sold its goods at cost. Assuming the company has booked its goods at historic cost, the profits will be artificially higher than the cash earnings. **Hence, in a rising inflationary environment, a constant EBITDA margin implies that the company has been underselling its goods as the real cost of goods sold is underestimated when booked in the P&L.**

Rising inflation and the banking sector: different sector, same dynamics

In a rising inflation environment, one might think that banks should be more protected than industrials. In theory, banks possess the ability to reprice investments after a few years (mortgages, e.g.) as the duration of their investments is low. However, as Santoni (The effects of inflation on commercial banks,

March 1986) demonstrated, **banks also get hit by rising inflation.** The mechanism is similar to that of industrials. **Stated earnings in a rising inflationary environment serves as a poor proxy for cash earnings.** For banks, the hidden cost is the charge brought to investors through the equity, for while loans and deposits grow in line with inflation, equity does not. Banks need to boost capital to maintain constant leverage as assets and liabilities rise with inflation. When analysing an annual report, one always gets the impression that both equity and net income grow in line with inflation. But for equity to grow at the same rate as assets, management must dedicate part of net income to equity capital. The dedicated amount equals the equity capital multiplied by the inflation rate. This charge does not go through the P&L—a bit like the treatment of share options a couple of years back—but it is a real cost to the investor and should be removed from net income. Santoni provides an elegant analysis of these conditions, demonstrating that inflation is particularly harmful to banks when it is unexpected. '*The unexpected increase in the price level causes a proportional reduction in the exchange value of both nominal assets and liabilities in terms of real goods. Because banks are typically net creditors in nominal instruments, bank owners lose wealth when there is unanticipated* inflation' (1986, p. 17).

The hypothetical case for a bank that has been growing its assets, capital and income in line with inflation since 1960 is illustrated in Fig. 9.6. Just as for industrials, real earnings are significantly below reported earnings and one should expect a significant drop in *P/E* ratio as inflation rises, while the *P/E* ratio should rise when inflation falls.

The illusion of value and the shortfalls of *P/E* and *P/BV*

Having analysed the distortions that inflation creates, I use the second part of this chapter to focus on distortions in valuation ratios that are based on accounting data. It is of fundamental importance to go back to first

	1960	1965	1970	1975	1981	1990	2000	2010
CPI	1.50%	1.60%	5.90%	9.10%	10.40%	5.40%	3.40%	1.60%
Cumulative inflation rate	100	106.6	131.3	181.9	307.4	460.3	598.4	737.1
Equity capital	130.6	139.1	171.4	237.6	401.3	576.7	760	962.5
Net income	13.1	13.9	17.1	23.8	40.1	57.7	76	96.2
Infl. cost	1.9	2.2	9.5	19.9	37.7	29.6	24.8	15.6
Infl. adj net income	11.1	11.8	7.6	3.9	2.4	28	51.2	80.7
ROE	10%	10%	10%	10%	10%	10%	10%	10%
Infl. adj ROE	8.50%	8.40%	4.40%	1.60%	0.60%	4.90%	6.70%	8.40%

FIGURE 9.6 Selected P&L, cash flow and balance sheet data for a hypothetical US financial. *From the author.*

principles. What matters for investors is the cash they receive from their investments. The *P/E* ratio serves as a proxy for the price-to-cash earnings ratio, since it is cash earnings that drives prices. In the case of our hypothetical Company A, earnings and cash earnings values are known and investors want to pay a ratio of 15 × on the cash earnings (CE). It is therefore possible to deduce the *P/E* ratio resulting from putting a ratio of 15 × on the CE. Hence one can answer the question: assuming that an investor wants to pay 15 × the cash earnings, what is the 'right' *P/E* ratio?

The data in Fig. 9.7 show that while the ratio of P/CE remains constant, the *P/E* ratio comes down until 1981. As cash earnings growth lags the pace of inflation, the share price lags the inflation rate during a rising inflationary environment for a company whose sales and profits are growing in line with inflation. In the example, between 1960 and 1981 both sales and net profits have an annual growth rate of 5.5% (in line with inflation), but the annual growth rate in cash earnings and share price is only 2.4% (Fig. 9.8). Other important implications are:

- **A stock that manages to grow its stated earnings and sales in line with inflation during a period of rising inflation should see a significant reduction in the *P/E* ratio.** Stated earnings overstate a company's real cash earnings. As the differential between stated earnings and cash earnings increases, *P/E* ratios contract.
- **A falling *P/E* ratio during a period of rising inflation does not correlate with a rising equity risk premium**. Fig.9.9 shows what the dynamics of the *P/E* ratio should have been for companies A, B and C, assuming a constant P/CE of 15 × between 1960 and 1981. There is an optical illusion of value based on *P/E*, but the P/CE is constant.

	1960	1965	1970	1975	1981	1991	2001	2010
Net profit	91.4	97.4	120.0	166.3	280.9	420.7	547.0	673.7
Cash earnings (CE)	77.4	84.7	89.7	98.7	127.0	269.2	418.2	540.7
Price to cash earn.s ratio	15x	15x	15x	15x	15x	15x	15x	15x
Theoretical price	1162	1271	1345	1481	1904	4039	6273	8111
Cum. P. appreciation	100	109.4	115.8	127.4	163.9	347.7	540.0	698.2
Cum. inflation rate	100	106.6	131.3	181.9	307.4	460.3	598.4	737.1
CPI	1.5%	1.6%	5.9%	9.1%	10.4%	4.2%	2.8%	1.6%
Implied fair level acc. P/E	12.7x	13.0x	11.2x	8.9x	6.8x	9.6x	11.5x	12.0x
Implied fair level P/B	1.42x	1.44x	1.36x	1.21x	1.02x	1.20x	1.34x	1.38x
Implied fair level infl adj P/B	1.24x	1.27x	1.09x	0.87x	0.66x	0.93x	1.11	1.17x

FIGURE 9.7 For a constant P/CE, *P/E* falls during times of rising inflation, but rises when inflation is declining. *From the author.*

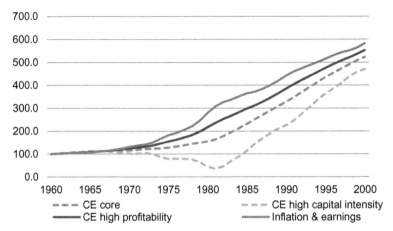

FIGURE 9.8 The dynamics of inflation, 'stated' earnings and 'cash earnings' for companies with different operational characteristics between 1960 and 2010. *From the author.*

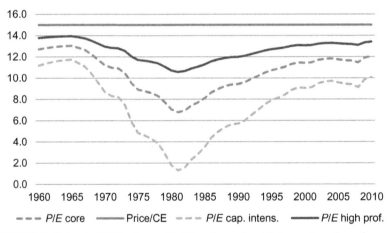

FIGURE 9.9 Fair value P/E for firms with different operational features. *From the author.*

- **The *P/E* ratio can be misleading when valuing companies in an infla-tionary environment.** Since the world of investment is obsessed with the *P/E* ratio and reported earnings, one tends to forget that stated earnings are only a proxy for cash earnings. In a low inflation environment, there is little difference between stated earnings and cash earnings. In an infla-tionary environment, the distance increases between stated earnings and cash earnings.
- **The best buying point for equities is not when the inflation rate is about to structurally rise, but when the inflation rate is about to structurally fall.** This is the tipping point for a sustained improvement in

cash returns and for cash earnings to grow at a faster pace than inflation. At this point, the *P/E* ratio is low; however, the low *P/E* is not an indication of value since in a constantly high inflation environment investors should expect a low *P/E* ratio.

The further risks of P/E relative

If inflation makes it risky to use the *P/E* ratio based on stated earnings, it is downright dangerous to use the reported *P/E* ratio when trying to compare companies with different levels of profitability or capital intensity, even within the same country. Take the examples of companies A, B and C. The company with the highest capital intensity (company B) appeared to be the most attractive in 1981, when it traded on a *P/E* ratio of $1.3 \times$. The others were trading at $6.9 \times$ and $10.9 \times$. Company B was on a *P/E* relative of 12%, so it certainly seemed a bargain. The harsh reality though is that the three stocks offered the same value to investors at the same P/CE of $15 \times$ (Fig. 9.9).

Ex post, the best investment in 1981 actually would have been the company on the lowest *P/E* ratio (based on stated earnings), but only because inflation was about to fall. That said, company B was also the one with the lowest *P/E* ratio in 1975, but as inflation ramped up between 1975 and 1981 investors would have seen cash earnings and prices go down by 60%. It is dangerous to use the *P/E* ratio when dealing with companies that have very different operational characteristics. In a rising inflationary environment the theory behind a constant *P/E* relative to the market dissolves completely, even for companies operating within the same country.

The practical limits of our hypothetical model: when companies are cheap on a real price-to-book and expensive on price-to-cash earnings

In our hypothetical model, I have assumed that the price will always follow cash earnings. If a company does not create any cash earnings, its price is zero. This does not happen in reality. Price follows cash earnings up to a point, and then the ratio of price-to-cash earnings starts to go up. This occurs when companies start to trade at a discount to the real capital invested and real returns on equity are very low.

In Appendix I share the example of Alcoa, which in 1981 was at an accounting *P/E* of $8 \times$ and a real *P/E* ratio of $212 \times$. Its real economic price-to-book was $0.3 \times$! The market was taking the view that only part of that business, and not much of it, was viable. Ultimately this contradiction should be put right: either returns should improve and the company becomes cheap compared to fair value or some of the assets should be written off. The worst outcome is that the company goes out of business. But, for a period of time, determining the real value of an investment can certainly be problematic.

Evidence confirms the hypotheses on how inflation impacts valuation

The evidence confirms that one should expect a fall in the *P/E* ratio in a period of rising inflation and a rise in the *P/E* ratio in a period of falling inflation.

Fig. 9.10 shows that stated earnings for the S&P 500 grew in line with inflation between 1960 and 1994. The compounded annual growth rate was 4.9% for inflation and 5.0% for earnings, which suggests that there was no real growth in earnings over the 34 years when inflation was high. As there was no real growth in earnings, one should observe a decrease in the *P/E* ratio when inflation is rising, which is precisely what happens (Fig. 9.11). As I mentioned before, this should not be taken as a measure of value but instead as an illustration that stated earnings are a poor proxy for cash earnings.

Data on cash earnings is limited to early 1980s

Ideally I would like to present data on cash earnings going back to the 1960s, but data on cash earnings only became available in the late 1970s. US companies only introduced a proper cash flow statement in 1987. Before that we had a 'Statement of Changes in Financial Position', introduced in 1971, which tracked companies in terms of either cash or working capital (the latter was more common). Proper cash flow statements came to the UK in 1991

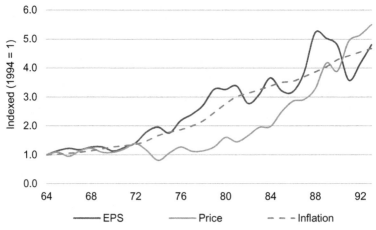

FIGURE 9.10   Cumulative growth of US inflation, and S&P 500 price and earnings, 1964−94. *Data from Bureau of Labor Statistics, S&P and Bloomberg Finance L.P.*

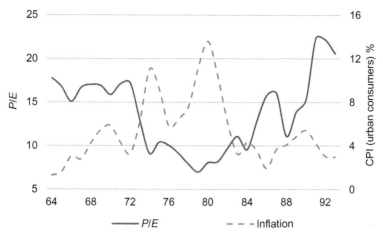

FIGURE 9.11   *P/E* ratio for the S&P 500, 1964—94. *Data from Bureau of Labor Statistics, S&P and Bloomberg Finance L.P.*

with FRS1. SSAP10 was introduced in the UK in 1975. Dubbed 'the statement of source and application of funds', it resembled its US equivalent.

Our sample of 21 US companies with data back to 1981 represents some of the largest companies in the market (EXXON, Chevron, Coca Cola, Johnson & Johnson, Wal-Mart). Our data are representative of current market valuations and, in my opinion, of the market in the early 1980s. Evidence from the sample is consistent with the model proposed in the report.

It is possible to see the accounting and real economic *P/E* for our sample of stocks in Fig. 9.12. There is a significant difference between the two, and the sample was trading at a real *P/E* ratio between $20 \times$ and $30 \times$, rather than below $10 \times$. The sample was cheap on economic price-to-book (Fig. 9.13), which makes sense given the low level of real cash returns. (see Fig. 9.14). Real returns are significantly below stated returns and the gap between the two narrows in the 1990s. In a nutshell, the assets were cheap in the early 1980s, but they did not generate much in the way of returns. The low real returns story in the early 1980s is consistent with Fig. 9.15, which shows the dividend yield for our sample and the free cash flow (FCF), a good proxy for CE ratio, once the dividend had been paid. The latter was mostly negative during the early 1980s, which suggests that firms were paying dividends by issuing debt rather than tapping their organic cash flow.

A recap of how inflation affects accounts and valuation

It is now clear that rising inflation hurts equities because inflation has negative effects on real profitability. When the growth in cash earnings is below

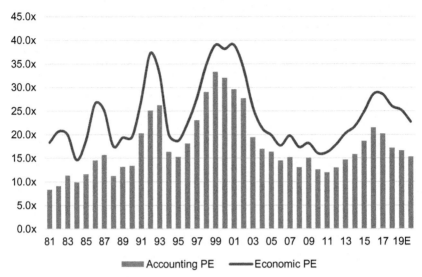

FIGURE 9.12 Accounting and economic *P/E* for selected US stocks. *Data from DWS and CROCI.*

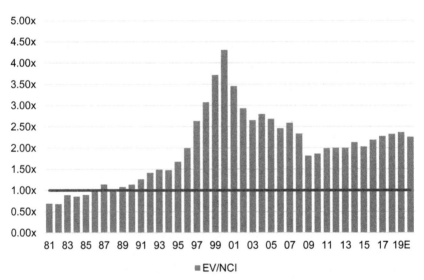

FIGURE 9.13 Economic price-to-book (EV/NCI). *Data from DWS and CROCI.*

inflation, profits and revenues that increase in line with inflation do not protect investors when inflation is rising. It is normal to think that when revenues and profits match inflation, investors are protected against the dangers of inflation. But this is wrong: an investor in a stock that grows its earnings in

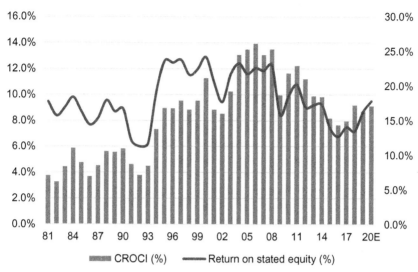

FIGURE 9.14 CROCI and ROE for selected US stocks. *Data from DWS and CROCI.*

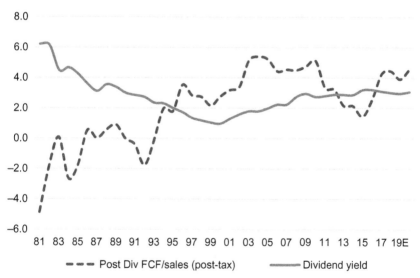

FIGURE 9.15 Dividend yield and post dividend free cash flow (FCF) ratio for selected US stocks. *Data from DWS and CROCI.*

line with inflation will not be protected because cash earnings grows below inflation.

Stated earnings are a poor proxy for cash earnings in a period of increasing inflation, whilst stated book underestimates the real value of the equity. As inflation rises, the gap between net profit margin and cash earnings margin widens. The opposite is true when inflation falls. To adjust the capital into today's money one must apply a cumulative multiplier of historical inflation (a function of the age of the assets).

Companies with high capital intensity suffer most when inflation is rising, and they benefit most as inflation starts falling in a structural manner. Companies with high levels of profitability suffer least as inflation rises, and they benefit least from falling inflation.

Increases in cash earnings outpace stated earnings growth during periods of falling inflation. Between 1981 and 2001, our core case saw revenues and profits up by 95%, but cash earnings was up by 229%. Cash earnings grows at a faster pace than stated earnings when inflation is falling and the delta between capex and depreciation comes down.

Companies need to increase EBITDA margins to offset the effects of inflation, as well as ensuring that net profit growth outpaces inflation. Cash earnings needs to grow in line with inflation. This is primarily due to an increase in real taxation and the impact of inflation on the value of goods sold. Taxation tends to increase in real terms as inflation rises. A constant reported EBITDA margin overstates the real EBITDA margin when inflation rises as some costs are booked in nominal terms.

Banks also suffer in an environment of rising inflation. The hidden charge brought to investors relates to equity; loans and deposits grow in line with inflation, but equity does not. As a result, a portion of net income needs to be allocated to equity to keep financial ratios constant. The stated and real ROE for US banks between 1960 and 2000 using the FDIC database and the methodology included in this report are shown in Fig. 9.17. The ROE is stable around 12%, decreasing in real terms until the late 1970s before starting to rise again.

In a rising inflationary environment stated returns go up whereas real returns come down; the opposite is true when inflation is falling. I call this 'the smile effect' of inflation on returns recorded in Fig. 9.16.

Implications for economists and academics

Most academic research about equities and inflation is based on the work of Modigliani and Cohn. In trying to understand why the P/E ratio fell between the 1960s and late 1970s, they considered the possibility that the P/E ratio should decrease as inflation rises but dismissed the hypothesis: '*We consider the possibility that the application of economically sound valuation methods decrees that the warranted price−earnings ratio (or, equivalently, the capitalisation factor to be applied to earnings) should systematically decrease with the rate of inflation. This would imply that even when earnings are keeping up with inflation, market values should decline in real terms − clearly a challenge to the traditional view that equity growth in nominal terms fully reflects the rate of inflation*'. (1979, pp. 24−25). In their view, if you grow earnings in line with inflation then the P/E ratio should be

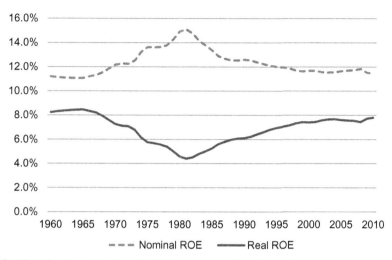

FIGURE 9.16 The smile effect of inflation on returns. *From the author.*

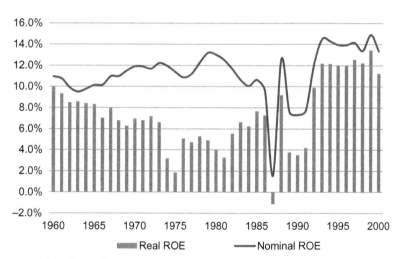

FIGURE 9.17 The smile effect of inflation on returns. *Data from Federal Deposit Insurance Corporation, DWS and CROCI.*

unchanged. But I have demonstrated that in an environment of rising inflation the earnings for a no-growth stock need to increase by more than inflation, the growth rate being a function of capital intensity and level of profitability. Otherwise, the *P/E* should decline, and its diminishing ratio cannot be seen as a measure of value.

Following the 1979 article, many academic researchers have argued that in periods of high inflation the stock market suffers from money illusion, discounting real cash flows at nominal rates. The implication, according to Modigliani and Cohn, is that equities become cheap when inflation rises.

The analysis in this chapter demonstrates that the *P/E* is not the price paid on real earnings, but instead the price paid on nominal earnings. A low *P/E* in an environment of high inflation is not a measure of real value; it is instead an indication that stated earnings are a poor proxy for cash earnings. **It is not so much that investors have been fooled by high inflation; rather, it seems that economists have been tricked.**

While Shiller's work in compiling the valuations of equities since 1881 is remarkable, it is also evident that economic rather than accounting data would be much more valuable. It is time to move away from the notion that markets were cheaply valued in the 1970s and early 1980s and focus on why markets appeared cheap even though in reality they were not.

Appendix

Real life examples from the early 1980s of how inflation distorted valuation

The early 1980s provide the best examples of markets not being attractively priced and equities being distorted by inflation. The inflation rate in the 1970s was so high that companies restated accounts by publishing supplementary (though unaudited) information describing the effects of general inflation. The following examples illuminate the damage inflation caused for equities. The most significant were delivered by depreciation. Some companies explained how taxation increased in real terms, and we note that the benefits that accrue to shareholders from a reduction in the value of debt do not offset higher real costs. Note how capital intensive businesses (Alcoa, International Paper, Exxon) were hit hardest in differences between stated and real assets and between stated and real profits. This is similar to what is described in the chapter.

EXXON

The effects of inflation on Exxon were brutal. Energy was the S&P's largest sector in the early 1980s, and Exxon's market cap was among the largest in the S&P500. The real book was more than twice the stated capital invested in the business. The stated ROE was close to 15%, but the real return was close to 0%. The positive impact of the devaluation of the debt was tiny in comparison to the real loss of earnings caused by inflation. The net effect was a real *P/E* ratio of around $200 \times$ versus an apparent *P/E* value of $6.0 \times$ (Fig. 9.18).

	As reported $m	Adjusted for general inflation $m
Net sales	103559	103559
Cost of sales	56084	57970
Depreciation	3333	5929
Net income as reported in the AR	4186	−296
Shareholders' equity	28440	69154
ROE	14.70%	NM
P/E (based on year end price)	6.04	NM
Saving on debt (mark to market)		557
Net income post mark to market of debt		126.6
Post mark to market PE ratio		200

FIGURE 9.18   Exxon, selected data from 1982 annual report. *Data from DWS, CROCI and company reports.*

	As reported ($m)	Adjusted for general inflation ($m)
Net sales	5033	5033
Cost of sales	3867	3878
Depreciation and depletion	297	514
Net income	238	9
Net assets	3137	6122
P/E	8.02	212
P/BV	0.61	0.31

FIGURE 9.19   Alcoa, selected data from 1981 annual report. *Data from DWS, CROCI and company reports.*

Alcoa

For Alcoa, another capital intensive business, adjusting for inflation resulted in a near doubling of the asset base and depreciation charge. Net earnings were eliminated (Fig. 9.19).

International Paper

In 1981 the management of International Paper talked about achieving savings by decreasing the nominal value of its debt. '*With the decline in the purchasing power of the dollar resulting from general inflation, the economic cost of repaying IP's debt has been reduced by about $122m*'. (AR, 1981, p. 35). These savings do not appear on the inflation-adjusted P&L; however, including their benefits would have pushed the real *P/E* from 95.4 × to 26.4 × versus a reported *P/E* of 3.9 × (Fig. 9.20).

	As reported ($m)	Adjusted for general inflation ($m)
Net sales	4983.4	4983.4
Cost of sales	3961	4004
Depreciation	223.4	365.9
Interest	37.3	37.3
Earnings before income taxes	777.5	299.1
Income taxes	252.5	252.5
Net income	525	46.6
Net assets	4440	7980
P/E (based on year end price)	3.9	95.4
Saving on debt (mark to market)		122
Post mark to market PE ratio		26.4

FIGURE 9.20 International Paper, selected data from 1981 annual report. *Data from DWS, CROCI and company reports.*

	As reported ($m)	Adjusted for general inflation ($m)
Net sales	5261	5261
Cost of sales	3292	3341
Depreciation and depletion	73	107
Net income	168	86
Net assets	1298	2096
P/E	8.15	15.96
P/BV	1.06	0.66

FIGURE 9.21 Colgate Palmolive, selected data from 1981 annual report. *Data from DWS, CROCI and company reports.*

Colgate

One might have expected the impact on a less capital-intensive business such as Colgate to have been less meaningful, but it is nevertheless noticeable. Colgate suffered from inflation through an increase in the cost of goods after adjusting its inventories to take account of inflation. The company used the LIFO method for over a quarter of its inventories (Fig. 9.21).

Pfizer

Pfizer pointed out that '*Of particular interest is the prohibition in SFAS 33 of restating the provision for taxes on income, thus highlighting the fact that under present tax laws the "costs" of inflation are not deductible and therefore act as a restraint to capital formation*'. It is also worth noting that the

	As reported ($m)	Adjusted for general inflation ($m)
Net sales	3750	3750
Cost of sales	1462	1480
Depreciation and depletion	115	179
Net income	447	365
Net assets	2181	2820
P/E	11.63	14.24
P/BV	2.38	1.84

FIGURE 9.22   Pfizer, selected data from 1983 annual report. *Data from DWS, CROCI and company reports.*

non-US portion of the business could be restated after currency translation, which would have altered the impact of inflation. Pfizer talked about the actions taken to minimise the problems caused by inflation, primarily involving cost reduction and cost avoidance as well as making some additions to improve capital productivity.

At the time each of these companies said how important productivity was to offsetting inflation. The issue today is starker: how can companies offset inflation through productivity improvements when the starting point for margins is so much higher? (Fig. 9.22).

Chapter 10

Bubbles in equities

Chapter Outline

Introduction

The very high level of equity return since the 2008 financial crisis and the strong performance of the technology sector often concern investors. Different competing theories have been advanced about bubble valuations in equities. Valuation bubbles are widely understood as a concept, but people cannot agree on a precise definition. Nobody can definitively describe why they form or how to spot them. Explanations of their sources vary from technological breakthroughs to the psychology of investors just getting carried away and suspending reason in the hopes of quick profit. A bubble normally begins with a paradigm shift where old processes or beliefs are considered obsolete. These paradigm shifts can follow various advances: access to new markets (the South Sea bubble), the introduction of new technologies (electricity and autos in 1920s; the internet in the late 1990s) and even liquidity, as may have been the case in specific areas after the 2009 financial crisis. The economic rationale for these new paradigms can often be sound. However, profits for early investors (in these paradigm shifts) catch the attention of additional participants who jump onto the bandwagon. Fear of missing out on an apparent once-in-a-lifetime opportunity grips the popular imagination, drawing in ever more participants. Prices skyrocket and eventually a full-blown asset bubble forms. In his book *Manias, Panics and Crashes*,[1] Charles Kindleberger describes a neat chronology of events leading to the formation of a bubble and its subsequent bust. This book draws on the work of another notable American economist, Hyman Minsky,

---

1. Kindleberger, C.P., 2000. Manias, Panics, and Crashes, A History of Financial Crises. Wiley Investment Classics.

Valuing and Investing in Equities. DOI: https://doi.org/10.1016/B978-0-12-813848-9.00010-8
         171

on credit cycles.[2] Kindleberger's book describes the five stages of a credit cycle that lead to a bubble[3]:

1. Displacement: This occurs when market participants are captivated by a new technology or development, encouraging them to believe that the future will be very different from the past.
2. Boom: Prices rise as participants enter the market in order to take advantage of the technology or development. This price rise attracts further participants who also want a piece of the action. The asset in question attracts wide media coverage, drawing ever more participants to the market.
3. Euphoria: Market activity reaches a state of extreme excitement. Caution is thrown to the wind. A greater fool theory plays out in the market, where market participants buy into the new asset with the expectation of selling it to someone else at a large profit. Valuations reach extreme levels during this stage, and prices lose their connections with fundamentals.
4. Profit-taking: Euphoria prepares the way for the subsequent reversal in prices. Smart money starts to leave the market as fundamentals fail to justify the prices even by the typically relaxed standards that prevail at this stage. Prices continue to rise even as upward momentum starts to fade. This stage continues until the market reaches a point where a sufficient number of participants lose faith in the rally. It will then only take a minor event to prick the bubble and prices start to deflate.
5. Panic: In this stage, asset prices descend rapidly. Falling prices result in margin calls which force leveraged participants to sell. This results in an even sharper drop in price and causes even the most determined participants to exit the market. A full-blown panic sets in, and prices fall as rapidly as they rose.

---

2. Hyman Minsky in his financial instability hypothesis described three kinds of financing. The first is 'Hedge financing' where companies rely on their future cash flows to repay all the borrowings. This is the safest form of financing. The other two, namely, 'Speculative financing' and 'Ponzi financing', are riskier. In the former, companies rely on their cash flows to repay interest but must roll over their debts to repay the principal. 'Ponzi financing' is the riskiest in which companies rely on additional debt to repay both the principal and the interest on existing debt. As companies' profitability falls, they progressively move from the 'hedge financing' end of Minsky's financing spectrum to the speculative and Ponzi end. This works for a while as, gripped by mania, market participants fail to heed to the deteriorating fundamentals. However, it reaches a point where the ongoing rally is no longer sustainable. At this stage it only takes a small event to reverse the course of prices.

3. Minsky, H., 1986. Stabilizing an Unstable Economy. McGraw-Hill Professional, New York.

Bubbles seen through CROCI's lens

The American economist James Tobin studied the relationship between the market value of assets and their replacement value.[4] Even though the ratio itself was introduced by Nicolas Kaldor, Tobin used it to demonstrate the relationship between market prices and economic activity. It is now popularly known as Tobin's Q:

$$\text{Econ. } \frac{P}{BV} = \text{Tobin's } Q = \frac{\text{Market value of assets}}{\text{Real replacement value of assets}}$$

The numerator of Tobin's Q is the market value of assets and the denominator is their replacement value. This is at the heart of CROCI process as well. CROCI includes all financial liabilities in its calculation of a company's market price, or EV. Similarly, all assets, including hidden assets, are included in CROCI's economic book value, or NCI. The latter is also adjusted for inflation, making NCI a good proxy for replacement value.

Tobin argued that there is a link between the market value of assets and economic activity. In periods where the market value of assets is below their replacement value (i.e. Tobin's Q below 1), there is little incentive for companies to invest. Every dollar of investment results in less than a dollar increase in market value. In these situations, it makes more sense for management to focus on starving the stock of assets of new capital and improving profitability. This process reduces the demand for goods and services, thereby reducing economic activity. The opposite happens when Tobin's Q or the EV/NCI is greater than 1. Every dollar of investment by a company is rewarded with an even higher increase in its market value. It makes sense for management to invest, resulting in higher demand for goods and services which then manifests as higher growth at the economy level.

Tobin's framework to measure bubbles in equities is evident, as the higher the Tobin's Q ratio, the higher the incentive to build assets for speculative purposes. The original model was applied to study the behaviour at the economy level. However, when applied to companies some adjustments are necessary to account for higher profitability at some companies. Tobin's model assumes that every company is a cost of capital business normally trading at a price-to-book ratio of one. In reality, levels of profitability vary and management typically considers the current level when making investments. A company that has a successful business delivering a return $5 \times$ the cost of capital should normally trade at $5 \times$ the capital. Evidence suggests that such companies will not normally invest in businesses that dilute their profitability. Therefore to assess speculative behaviour, I propose some adjustments to the model and to Tobin's arguments. Instead of analysing such behaviour

---

4. Tobin, J., Brainard, W.C., 1976. Asset Markets and the Cost of Capital. Economic Progress, Cowles Foundation, Yale University.

when the price-to-book ratio is above one, it ought to take place when it is above the existing level of profitability. This means that the incentive to build takes place when:

$$\frac{EV}{NCI} > \frac{CROCI}{COC} \text{ rather than } \frac{EV}{NCI} > 1$$

Measuring the EV/NCI is fairly straightforward, as one can find information about the market price and the capital invested. The challenge is to measure the level of cash return (CROCI). Spot cash return can be misleading, especially in cyclical companies where value can be depressed in a recession year. We take a smoothed measure instead of using an average over a period of time (5 years, although we have also analysed it by using cash returns over 10 years). Companies with cash returns below 3% are excluded, as the ratio can become distorted with small denominators. For the cost of capital, we take the market-implied cost of capital (discount rate, see Chapter 4: Stock picking based on economic fundamentals) as a representation of what investors demand to provide capital at risk.

Over the long term, the EV/NCI tends to track underlying profitability. However, variations are possible due to growth and fade factors. Growth companies normally have a higher EV/NCI and markets expect the company to keep on growing their capital (NCI) in the foreseeable future, which will mathematically result in a lower EV/NCI ratio. Fading, or troubled, companies see a decline in their levels of profitability. The ratio has some challenges, but they should not be overstated. First, our focus is on medium, large and megacaps, and so growth rates are generally not too high; second, we ensure that companies have 5 entire years of operations so we can measure the 5-year average CROCI third, we define the 'bubble' as a level significantly higher than the company's previously achieved levels.

Our bubble taxonomy has four categories. The first category is a 'fair value' category. It assumes that companies seldom trade exactly in line with profitability. For much of the time, a small premium or discount exists because of volatility in share price and/or changing expectations about future profitability. Within our proprietary taxonomy, if the company trades within 10% of its long-term valuation, we deem the company 'fairly valued'. If the company is trading at a 10%–50% premium to valuation, we call it 'overvalued/expensive'. When the current economic price-to-book value (EV/NCI) is more than $1.5 \times$ the 5-year average CROCI, the company is in 'bubble' territory. This implies a 50% premium over the levels justified by profitability. The last category is made up of companies pricing a structural decline in profitability, that is pricing a long-term return at least 30% below the 5-year average.

Bubbles can form at the market level or they can remain isolated in individual companies or sectors. With the benefit of hindsight it is easy to spot bubbles, such as the share price of Coca-Cola in the late 1990s. Strong operational performance in the late 1980s caused market participants to become overly optimistic about Coca-Cola's future prospects. Prices eventually became detached from profitability, leading to overvaluation in the early 1990s. A period of introspection ensued, but continued improvements in profitability challenged investors' suspicions and in 1994 prices started to rise rapidly. During the next 4 years the economic price-to-book (EV/NCI) of Coca-Cola rose from just under $3 \times$ the cost of capital to $6.8 \times$. Market participants who were invested in the stock during this period would have seen more than a fourfold increase in the value of their investments. However, as with any other bubble, the period of overexcitement did not last. As profitability plateaued, prices fell sharply at first and then continued downward for the next 7 years. Market participants who remained invested for the whole period would have seen the values of their investments halve from their peaks (Fig. 10.1).

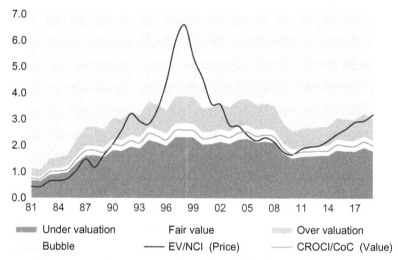

FIGURE 10.1 Coca-Cola bubble. *Data from DWS and CROCI.*

Bubbles themselves are not hazardous, but investors would benefit from knowing when to exit. This is not an easy task by any means. Investors may struggle to time their exits, but staying out of the market in the early stages of a bubble may not be ideal either. The latter is especially true for broad asset class bubbles. As John Maynard Keynes famously said, 'The market can remain irrational for longer than you can remain solvent'.

Microsoft's valuation history is also intriguing. By 2000, the company was delivering a return that was $14 \times$ the cost of capital, but the stock at its highest point was trading on $70 \times$ the level of capital invested (Fig. 10.2).

As Microsoft was a growth stock, I rearrange the previous equation.

$$EV \times COC > CROCI \times NCI \quad \text{rather than} \quad \frac{EV}{NCI} > \frac{CROCI}{COC}$$

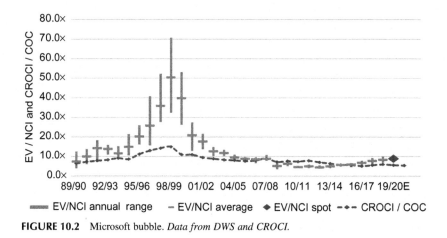

FIGURE 10.2 Microsoft bubble. *Data from DWS and CROCI.*

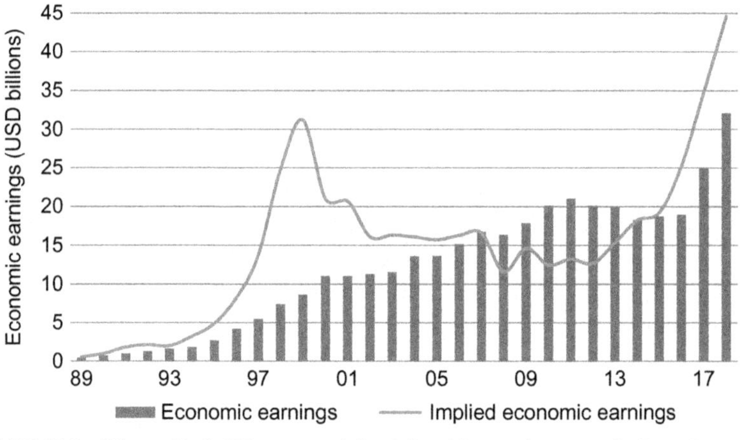

FIGURE 10.3 Microsoft's bubble was partially deflated by earnings growth. *Data from DWS and CROCI.*

The rearrangement allows me to compare the actual levels of economic earnings with the levels implied by the share price. The result can be seen in Fig. 10.3. The chart shows two sets of data. The bars indicate the level of economic earnings as measured in 2019 currency (this is done in order to remove the potential effects of inflation, which would normally show that earnings are growing). The line is the average sustainable level of earnings in perpetuity priced by the market. Between 1989 and 2000, Microsoft grew its earnings but expectations about its sustainable level of earnings went up as the market became convinced that Microsoft would grow earnings further and sustain them. The bubble that inflated during the dot-com bubble was

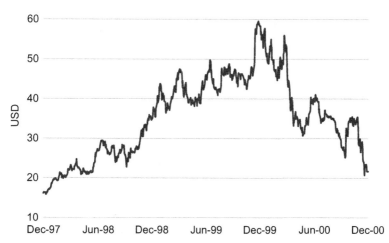

FIGURE 10.4   Microsoft share price. *Reproduced with permission from Bloomberg Finance L.P.*

partially deflated when the share price troughed at the end of 2000. Thereafter, the growth in earnings increased the denominator of the Economic P/E, in turn reducing the valuation. By 2007/2008, market valuations were in line with Economic Profits. By 2012, the stock was pricing a structural fall in profitability. Between 2011 and 2014, the level of earnings decreased, but the stock started to rerate as the market and analysts repriced Microsoft as a growth stock. This chart beautifully illustrates the importance of emotion and psychology in market dynamics. Markets might be efficient in the medium term, but psychology and emotion play a fundamental role in equity markets (Fig. 10.4).

Bubbles can result in boom and bust cycles

Not all valuation bubbles bring about higher levels of investment. Coca-Cola is a good example. However, bubbles often beget increased investments, and this situation can quickly become dangerous at the market or sector level.

Higher economic activity fuelled by higher asset prices often leads investors, company management and even regulators into believing that things are progressing along the right path. However, at the micro-level, cracks appear that can ultimately lead to a reverse in prices or even end in a bust. Fig. 10.5 depicts the level of capital invested in the Communication Equipment sector since 1989. Fig. 10.6 shows the Economic Profits generated by the sector (the vertical bars) and the profits priced by the market (the dark line). Between 1989 and 2000 there were steady increases in both capital and earnings. Until 1997 investors just assumed that these earnings were sustainable,

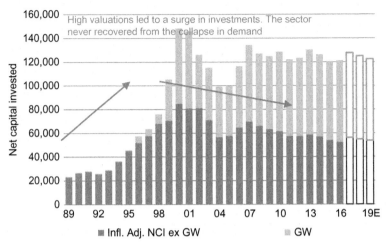

FIGURE 10.5   Net capital invested in the Communications Equipment sector (USD mn). *Data from DWS and CROCI. The chart only includes companies for which CROCI has comparable data going back to 1989.*

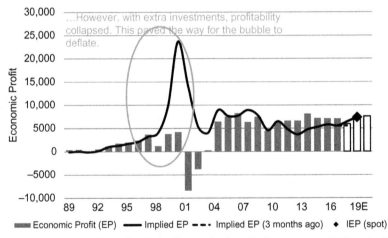

FIGURE 10.6   Economic Profits of the Communications Equipment sector (USD mn). *Data from DWS and CROCI. The chart only includes companies for which CROCI has comparable data going back to 1989.*

but after 1998 the market's expectations shot up, and put higher and higher prices on the earnings. There also was a bout of speculation in the telecoms sector, and when it eventually collapsed it dragged down the entire telecom equipment sector. Capital had to be written off, and the sector took ages of restructuring to recover.

Equity bubble at the end of 2018 and implications

Bubble economics are notoriously controversial. Nobel laureate Eugene Fama argues that talking about bubbles is largely irrelevant since it is impossible to forecast them. Of course, he is factually correct. When markets are expensive, investors in large diversified benchmarks effectively demand a low expected rate of return. Bubbles do not exist because, in Fama's model, they are not economic events worth worrying about. *In the world of efficient markets, price equals value and stock picking is irrelevant; what matters is risk and return. This should not be the case for fundamental investors, academics and policymakers.* Analysts that are concerned about fundamentals, buy companies when they know the difference between price and value. Academics ought to provide an understanding of market dynamics. Policymakers need to define policies that avoid boom and bust by monitoring and understanding the prices of assets (equities, in particular).

Inflating asset prices into bubble territory is not necessarily a bad thing. Significant amounts of wealth are generated during the formation of bubbles. There are economic benefits too when higher risk appetites drive investment. However, risks develop when growing appetites create an artificial (unsustainable) demand for a good or service. Further investments driven by a high price-to-capital ratio tend to result in excess capacity that undermines long-term profitability and equity prices. To improve the investment process and economic policies, there needs to be a better appreciation of the associated risks. Quantitative easing was about inflating assets. How can such an approach be justified if the price cannot be compared to the level justified by valuation?

For nearly two decades, we have been monitoring potential equity bubbles using our economic valuation framework. At the end of 2018, we were able to say:

- The ratio of stocks in bubble territory was at the same level in 2018 as it was in 2000 (Fig. 10.7).
- The level of overvaluation in 2018 was smaller on average than in 2000 (Fig. 10.8). This is another way of saying that there were as many bubbles but that they were smaller.
- Japan had the highest proportion of bubbles in 2000 but the smallest proportion in 2018. In the United States, there were more bubbles in 2018 than there were in 2000 (Fig. 10.9).
- Back in 2000, IT, Healthcare, Energy and Communication dominated the landscape. These have now been replaced by Consumer Staples (higher than 50%) and Utilities. Industrials and Consumer Discretionary registered the lowest proportion of companies in bubble valuation (Fig. 10.10).

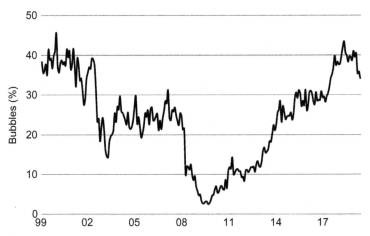

FIGURE 10.7 Proportion of companies globally in bubbles. *Data from DWS and CROCI.*

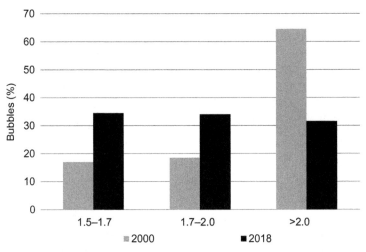

FIGURE 10.8 Distribution of global bubble valuation. *Data from DWS and CROCI.*

The proportion of companies in bubble territory at the end of 2018 was comparable to 2000, but the size of the bubble (proportion of companies with relative valuation above 2×) is much smaller. This suggests that central banks have been successful in reflating assets post-2009, which is an interesting indicator in the current (September 2019) debate about how much the Fed ought to cut interest rates. It is also evident that low interest rates have created a situation where a significant number of Utilities and Staples companies were in bubble valuation at the end of 2018. Nevertheless, because of very strong growth in earnings in IT and Healthcare, the

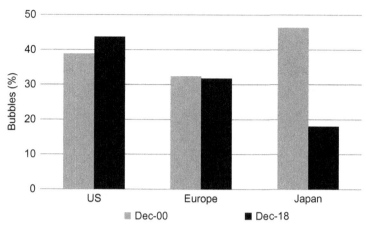

FIGURE 10.9   Bubbles by region. *Data from DWS and CROCI.*

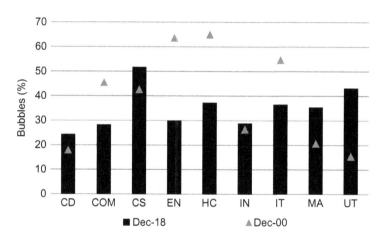

FIGURE 10.10   Bubbles by sector. *Data from DWS and CROCI.*

proportion of companies in these sectors in bubble territory is significantly below the levels seen in 2000. I cannot fail to think that practitioners, academics and policymakers would benefit from a systematic framework on bubbles in equities. But perhaps I have spent too much time analysing the world from the bottom-up.

Chapter 11

Odysseus on valuing and investing in equities

Chapter Outline

By chance, writing this book coincided with a sailing holiday in the Ionian islands of Greece, close to my home. Rereading the Odyssey, the second-oldest extant work of Western literature and a cornerstone of the Western canon, was a must. 'History does not repeat itself but it often rhymes', Mark Twain reputedly said. Homer's epic is a wonderful narrative about struggle, as valid today as it was over 2800 years ago. Odysseus was away from home for 20 years. He was at war in Troy for 10 years and it took him another 10 to return to his home in Ithaca. When he finally arrived, instead of a welcoming party he was met by a new challenge. During his journey, nothing was as it seemed, and his adventures became fights of determination and belief. One can easily relate to the very colourful situations described in its 24 books. In fact, the Odyssey has been used as a reference for a number of CROCI annual outlooks.[1]

CROCI will soon celebrate its 25th anniversary. Since its inception, it has been a fight of determination and belief. There are certainly many colourful histories that can be told, and some have been described by Pascal in his book, but the most interesting story has yet to be written. Our understanding of equities is still in the making.

As I am writing the concluding remarks to this book (September 2019), many investors are about to give up on value stocks after another *annus horribilis* so far in 2019. However, this is not the sole challenge. More than 30% of fixed income investments have negative interest. Think of a situation

---

1. CROCI Outlook 2017, 'A Happy Odyssey', CROCI Outlook 2018, 'The Siren Song', CROCI Outlook 2019, 'Scylla and Charybdis'.

Valuing and Investing in Equities. DOI: https://doi.org/10.1016/B978-0-12-813848-9.00011-X
© 2020 Elsevier Inc. All rights reserved.

where you have two people, one with financial capital and the other needing it. The latter says. *give me $100 and within 10 years I will give you $99*. Absurd? Think again. In August 2019, Jyske Bank in Denmark launched the first 10-year mortgage with a −0.5% rate.[2]

We are also witnessing significant changes in the way investors behave. For example, environmental, social and governance (ESG) investing is a clear step along the path of investment democratisation. In the past, the consumer simply had to trust the institution behind the product. We now live in a world of increasing scrutiny about how and why consumers' capital is used. ESG is not a fad; rather, it heralds greater consumer activism and demands for transparency in the investment process.

If, as it seems, the world economy is moving to a period of slower economic growth, then investors are likely to earn lower returns. They will scrutinise their investments more closely and demand higher levels of service from the custodians of their investments. Forty years ago, the consumer needed to go to a physical branch to buy an equity product or stocks, and an asset management company was responsible for creating the products and delivering the service at the branch. I foresee a future in which the consumer has the ability to amass information about each listed stock and assemble a portfolio that meets her requirements at her fingertips. New technologies such as blockchain will disrupt the value chain, creating new winners and losers among financial institutions.

The end of this chapter lists the principal views and findings of this book. Knowledge is bounded by our limited rationality as well as by our historic context, so some of these principles will evolve. This is why valuing and investing in equities is a social science. However, there will always be a Real Investor, who thinks that when buying equities, she is buying a piece of a company. This is the person that this book has been written for. Hopefully you have enjoyed the book as much as I have enjoyed writing it.

Twenty years of CROCI fundamental analysis in four pages

Investors

- Clearly define which type of investor you wish to be (on the typology scale). Your choice will define your investment process: first, the balance between pure valuation and pure price; second, how much emphasis must be placed on the benchmark.
- Many investors are speculators in disguise: they are primarily interested in price and price dynamics. The Real Investor equates purchasing equities with buying whole companies and is aware of the difference between

---

2. The Guardian, 13 August 2019, 'Danish bank launches world's first negative interest rate mortgage'.

value and price. When using concepts such Real Value, Real Price and Real Capital, I am referring to a process that serves this hypothetical investor.

- There are stock pickers, buying and holding stocks for the medium to long term. There are also investors who can use a real investment process to run an intelligent systematic investment process.

The investment process

- Investing in equities is challenging. It is one of the few asset classes where prices are driven by two factors, earnings and the discount rate, and both can change.
- The fundamental formula for investors is: *Financial Capital* × *Financial Return* = *Operational Capital* × *Operational Return.* On one side of the equation are the investors with capital and its associated return requirements; on the other side is the company with its operating capital (financed by investors), which generates a return. Investment is about this simple equation, and every sound valuation ratio is just a rearrangement of it. Fundamental valuation is about understanding and analysing the components of this equation.
- There are always two sides in an investment process (the investor and the company) and it is essential to look at capital and return from both sides.
- There is a dark side and a bright side to valuation. The dark side is about understanding the dynamics of investor behaviour (their willingness to provide financial capital and the return they expect). The bright side is about understanding the balance sheet and the return on capital.
- The starting point of the real investment process ought to be the balance sheet. You are in effect buying a piece of a listed company, so you must look at the assets you want to purchase.
- Estimating the future dynamics of a business is an art rather than a science.
- Fundamental analysis is a rich source for thematic investing.
- Adjustments to valuation have to be consistent over time, as the real investment process needs to transcend fads and fashions.

Due diligence

- Performing due diligence on accounts matters. The median impact on valuation of CROCI's adjustments at the end of 2018 was 50%, but it can sometimes be as much as 350%. Some companies can also be up to 80% cheaper than they appear to be.
- The market can make implicit adjustments to the valuation of certain low cash conversion companies by putting them on low (conventional)

valuations. This may confuse some investors who will fail to distinguish between apparent cheapness and genuine value.

- Performing due diligence on companies can be a painful process. A Real Investor should never compromise: better to have no opinion on a company if there are concerns over its disclosure or governance than to take unnecessary risks.
- There are two types of value trap that investors should avoid. First, perform a full due diligence on the company's accounts. Second, judge the sustainability of the business and its profitability.
- Company analysis ought to be an assessment of the business by focusing on the real level of earnings and specifically on its drivers, capital and returns (Chapter 4, Stock picking based on economic fundamentals).

Valuations

- The closer on the spectrum to a Type 1 investor you are, the more important valuation becomes. Type 1 investors should be happy to spend 100% of their time on due diligence. A Type 3 investor (e.g. one combining value and momentum) will have to compromise and use inferior valuation ratios or a simplified process.
- There are four broad classes of adjustment to be made to companies: capturing total financial liabilities, inflation, hidden assets and the economic life of capital.
- Financials is the only sector with a genuinely different discount rate. That rate is inflated because of the significantly higher risk associated with owning the equity.
- Financials is one of the few sectors with nominal assets, and so an inflation adjustment ought to be made to the flow as investors face the cost of keeping equity growth in line with inflation.
- Once you have an adjusted valuation, you can compare companies and their valuations without needing to worry about which sector or country they are in.
- Within our large/mid cap coverage, most risk premia concepts are artificial constructs that address academics' inability to perform due diligence on companies.
- When measured properly, value does not necessarily have a higher risk profile.
- If you are concerned about the sustainability of a business, you may adjust valuation for risk, as measured by volatility.
- The valuation of equities was distorted in the late 1970s and 1980s by the high level of inflation. Markets were much more expensive than they appeared to be.

Accounting-based valuations

- Be sceptical of accounting-based valuation ratios for any kind of analysis (including academic research) as what you see is not necessarily what you get.
- Accounts are not created for equity investors.
- Be aware of the shortcomings of the various accounting ratios, especially EV/EBITDA.
- For a purist, the concept of value cannot be built on accounting valuation ratios.
- The concept of real valuation does not fit well with accounting data. Instead, value should be measured through a proper economic framework.
- It is normal to expect an accounting-based P/E ratio to fall when inflation rises, as earnings are a poor proxy for the real level of cash earnings. Conversely it is normal to expect a rise in the nominal P/E ratio when inflation is falling, as the P/E ratio can serve as a better proxy for the real level of cash earnings.

Investment strategies

- Concentrated value strategies deliver the best long-term return, but it can be a rocky ride. We call this the 'à la Buffet' approach. You may decide to minimise tracking error versus a benchmark, but that is no longer a pure stock-picking approach.
- Dividends are an important component of equity returns, but do not think that purely high dividend strategies are value strategies. Substantial risk exists in high dividend yield strategies, and they generally contain insufficient real economic value. For dividend-focused investors, more attractive strategies remove unnecessary risks such as high leverage, low profitability and high volatility.
- A systematic analysis of CROCI-based factors suggests that value is the best factor in delivering performance to long-term investors. quality (CROCI), volatility and financial leverage are factors that help reduce risk. Intangible intensity is not an alpha factor.
- Real Investors looking for broad equity exposure ought to invest in equities based on real earnings weighting.
- Companies investing in intangible capital (R&D and Brands) have recently started to drive economic growth.
- Our knowledge of financial markets continues to grow, given that investing in equities as a mass consumer phenomenon started only about 50 years ago.
- Beware of the confusing framework created by major index providers.

- Contrary to the academic consensus, inflation does not fool equity investors. The same cannot always be said for academics.
- Bubbles do not exist in the world of the efficient market hypothesis (EMH) because that world recognises no difference between price and value. Its adherents are not stock pickers, and when markets are expensive investors simply receive a low rate of return. From this viewpoint, bubbles are economically irrelevant.
- Bubbles do exist and can be measured.

Much academic research on equity markets still remains to be done. Too many articles continue to use misleading accounting data, which hampers their conclusions. Capital and return are the foundation of our capitalist system, and a better understanding of equities for both professionals and laymen is not just desirable but necessary.

Bibliography

Adorno, T.W., 1978. (EFN Jephcott trans. Ed.) Minima Moralia: Reflections on a Damaged Life. Verso.

Akerlof, G.A., Shiller, R.J., 2009. Animal Spirits – How Human Psychology Drives the Economy, and Why It Matters for Global Capitalism. Princeton University Press.

Ancell, K., 2012. The Origin of the First Index Fund. University of Chicago Booth School of Business.

Arnott, R.D., Hsu, J., Moore, P., 2005. Fundamental indexation. Financial Analysts Journal.

Barry, R., 2014. Crisis and Complexity, Volume I – An Inquiry into the Nature and Causes of Economic and Financial Crisis. First Principles Pty Ltd.

Berger, T., Frey, C.B., 2016a. Technology, Globalisation and the Future of Work in Europe: Essays On Employment in a Digitised Economy. Oxford Martin Programme on Technology & Employment.

Berger, T., Frey, C.B., 2016b. Structural Transformation in the OECD. OECD Publishing, p. 13.

Bernstein, P.L., 2005. Capital Ideas – the Improbably Origins of Modern Wall Street. John Wiley & Sons, Inc, Hoboken, New Jersey.

Bogle, J.C., 2013. The Clash of the Cultures: Investment Vs. Speculation. John Wiley & Sons.

Bootle, R., 2003. Money for Nothing – Real Wealth, Financial Fantasies and the Economy of the Future. Nicholas Brealey Publishing.

Bouchey, P., Nemtchinov, V., Paulsen, A., Stein, D.M., 2012. Volatility harvesting: why does diversifying and rebalancing create portfolio growth? J. Wealth Manag.

Buffet W., 2008. Berkshire Hathaway Annual report.

Carroll, L., 1865a. Alice's Adventures in Wonderland. MacMillan and Co.

Carroll, L., 1865b. Through the Looking-Glass, and What Alice Found There. MacMillan and Co.

Chow, T.-m, Hsu, J., Kalesnik, V., Little, B., 2011. A survey of alternative equity index strategies. Financial Anal. J.

Costantini, P., 2006. Cash Return on Capital Invested: Ten Years of Investment Analysis with the CROCI Economic Profit Model. Butterworth-Heinemann.

Damodaran, A., 2011. The Little Book of Valuation. John Wiley and Sons.

Downing, J., Reamer, N., 2016. Investment: A History. Columbia Business School Publishing.

El-Erian, M.A., 2008. When Markets Collide: Investment Strategies for the Age of Global Economic Change. McGraw-Hill Education.

Fama, E., 2017. Journal of Applied Corporate Finance 28 (4), John Wiley and Sons.

Fama, E.F., French, K.R., 1992. The cross-section of expected stock returns. J. Financ. 47 (2).

Fama, E.F., French, K.R., 1996. Multifactor explanations of asset pricing anomalies. Journal of Finance 51 (1).

Fernholz, R., 1995. Portfolio Generating Functions. INTECH Investment Management.

Frey, C.B., Osborne, M.A., 2013. The Future of Employment: How Susceptible are Jobs to Computerisation. Oxford Martin School.

Goos, M., Manning, A., Salomons, A., 2014. Explaining job polarization: routine-biased technological change and offshoring. Am. Econ. Rev. 104 (8), 2509–2526.

Graham, B., 1973. Intelligent Investor: the Definitive Book on Value Investment, fourth revised edition Harper & Row.

Graham, B., Dodd, D.L., 2009. Security Analysis – Sixth Edition, First Edition 1934 McGraw-Hill.

Greenblatt, J., 2006. The Little Book that Beats the Market. John Wiley & Sons, Inc, Hoboken, New Jersey.

Haskel, J., Westlake, S., 2018. Capitalism Without Capital – the Rise of the Intangible Economy. Princeton University Press.

Homer, The Odyssey, 8th century B.C. (approx.)

Keynes, J.M., 1931. Economic Possibilities for Our Grandchildren, Essays in Persuasion. Harcourt Brace.

Kindleberger, C.P., 2000. *Manias, Panics and Crashes*: A History of Financial Crises. Wiley Investment Classics (first published Norton, 1978).

Marathon Asset Management Limited, 2004. Copyright © 2004 by Capital Account – A Money Manager's Reports on a Turbulent Decade 1993-2002. Marathon Asset Management Limited (Marathon-London in the USA), Texere, part of the Thomson Corporation.

Minksy, H., 1986. Stabilizing an Unstable Economy. McGraw-Hill Professional, New York.

Minsky, H.P., 1992. The Financial Instability Hypothesis. Levy Economics Institute.

Modigliani, F., Miller, M.H., 1958. The cost of capital, corporation finance and the theory of investment. Am. Econ. Rev. 48 (3), Published by American Economic Association.

Modigliani, F., Cohn, R.A., 1979. Inflation, rational valuation and the market. Financials Analysts Journal 35, 24–44.

Pacioli L., 1494. Summa de arithmetica, geometria. proportioni et proportionalita. Paganini (Venice).

Perlis, A., 1982. Epigrams on programming. Artic. ACM SIGPLAN J.

Piketty, T., 2013. Capital in the Twenty-First Century. Harvard University Press.

Reamer, N., Downing, J., 2016. Investment, a History. Columbia Business School Publishing.

Retail Gazette, 24th December 2018. <https://www.retailgazette.co.uk/blog/2018/12/150000-high-street-jobs-lost-2018/>.

Santoni, G.J., 1986. The Effects of Inflation on Commercial Banks. Economic Research, Federal Reserve Bank of St. Louis.

Schwab, K., 2016. The Fourth Industrial Revolution. World Economic Forum.

Shiller, R.J., 2005. Irrational Exuberance, Second Edition Princeton University Press.

Siegel, J.J., 1998. Stocks for the Long Run – Second Edition, Revised and Expanded. McGraw-Hill, First Published 1994.

Spier, G., 2014. The Education of a Value Investor: My Transformative Quest for Wealth, Wisdom, and Enlightenment. St Martin's Press.

Stewart III, G.B., 1991. The Quest for Value. HarperCollins Publishers, Inc.

Susskind, R., Susskind, D., 2015. The Future of the Professions – How Technology will Transform the Work of Human Experts. Oxford University Press.

Thaler, R.H., 2015. Misbehaving – The Making of Behavioural Economics. Penguin Random House, UK.

Tobin, J., Brainard, W.C., 1976. Asset Markets and the Cost of Capital. Economic Progress, Cowles Foundation, Yale University.

Wilde, O., 1893. Lady Windermere's Fan. Elkin Mathews, John Lane at The Sign of the Bodley Head in Vigo Street.

Index

Printed in the United States
By Bookmasters